Charles Darwin

VIP
Very Interesting People

Bite-sized biographies of Britain's most
fascinating historical figures

Charles Darwin

Very Interesting People VIP

Adrian Desmond,
James Moore,
and Janet Browne

OXFORD
UNIVERSITY PRESS

OXFORD
UNIVERSITY PRESS

Great Clarendon Street, Oxford ox2 6DP

Oxford University Press is a department of the University of Oxford.
It furthers the University's objective of excellence in research, scholarship,
and education by publishing worldwide in

Oxford New York

Auckland Cape Town Dar es Salaam Hong Kong Karachi
Kuala Lumpur Madrid Melbourne Mexico City Nairobi
New Delhi Shanghai Taipei Toronto

With offices in

Argentina Austria Brazil Chile Czech Republic France Greece
Guatemala Hungary Italy Japan Poland Portugal Singapore
South Korea Switzerland Thailand Turkey Ukraine Vietnam

Oxford is a registered trade mark of Oxford University Press
in the UK and in certain other countries

Published in the United States
by Oxford University Press Inc., New York

First published in the *Oxford Dictionary of National Biography* 2004
This paperback edition first published 2007

© Oxford University Press 2007

Database right Oxford University Press (maker)

First published 2007

British Library Cataloguing in Publication Data

Data available

Library of Congress Cataloging in Publication Data

Data available

Typeset by SPI Publisher Services, Pondicherry, India
Printed in Great Britain
on acid-free paper by
Ashford Colour Press Ltd, Gosport, Hants.

ISBN 978–0–19–921354–2 (Pbk.)

10 9 8 7 6 5 4 3 2 1

Contents

Preface

So vast and various was Charles Darwin's life that his first biographer required three 400-page tomes to tell it. That *Life and Letters of Charles Darwin* (1887), edited by his son Francis, is still the starting-point for Darwinian biographical reflection. Why then, in the twenty-first century, has it taken three collaborators to produce this modest life, originally written for the *Oxford Dictionary of National Biography* and the Dictionary's only triple-authored entry?

Darwin Studies grow larger by the day. Darwin was the 'compleat naturalist', his interests and publications ranging across disciplines that have become whole specialist fields. After decades of intense scholarship, historians now know more about his career than his family did, and in respects—given the fifteen huge volumes of *The Correspondence of Charles Darwin* already published (with seventeen still to come)—they even know more of the man. Having almost a hundred years of Darwin-related research between the three of us, we have managed the unwieldy subject by triangulating from different sides. This slim book gives a composite portrait.

Our perspectives are complementary. Adrian Desmond has specialized on Victorian views of fossils and the politics of evolution in the 1830s; on Darwin's heretical teacher Robert Grant and later proselytizer T. H. Huxley. Jim Moore collaborated with Desmond on *Darwin* (1991), and is doing so again (2006) for a book about the anti-slavery background to Darwin's theories on human origins. Moore himself, with backgrounds in physical science, divinity and church history, has written on the social and theological contexts of Darwin's career, about religious responses to his theories and the making of his posthumous reputation. Janet Browne, a historian of biology, has studied Darwin's botany, illness and iconography, and published a two-volume biography *Charles Darwin* (1995–2002).

No longer the timeless genius of nineteenth- and twentieth-century scientific hagiography, the Darwin we introduce is richly embedded in the social, political–economic and religious life of his age. With his face on the British ten-pound note, Darwin's familiarity is assured. But the range of his interests is less well known; and so we have discussed his *Beagle* voyage, barnacles and botany, geology and politics, theology and family as sustaining and essential to his life-dominating line of research on natural selection. It was this wide-ranging evolutionary work that had such social impact and put much of the wonder into what Victorians called the 'Wonderful Century'.

Adrian Desmond,
James Moore, and Janet Browne
August 2006

About the authors

Adrian Desmond is an Honorary Research Fellow in the Biology Department at University College London. His books include *The Politics of Evolution* (1989) and the two-volume *Huxley* (1994–7).

James Moore is Professor of the History of Science at the Open University and author of *The Post-Darwinian Controversies* (1979), *The Darwin Legend* (1994), and *Darwin* (1991) with Adrian Desmond.

Janet Browne is Professor of the History of Science at Harvard University. Her books include the two-volume *Charles Darwin* (1995–2002) and *The Origin of Species: A Biography* (2006).

Upbringing and education

Charles Robert Darwin (1809–1882), naturalist, geologist, and originator of the theory of natural selection, was born on 12 February 1809 at The Mount, Shrewsbury, the fifth child and second son of Robert Waring Darwin (1766–1848), Shrewsbury's principal physician, and Susannah Wedgwood (1765–1817). His sisters were Marianne, Caroline, Susan, and Emily Catherine, his brother Erasmus Alvey. His grandfathers, the potter Josiah Wedgwood (1730–1795) and the evolutionist poet and physician Erasmus Darwin (1731–1802), were leading lights of the industrial revolution; his grandmothers were respectively Sarah Wedgwood (1734–1815) and Mary Howard (1740–1770). Charles's mother died in 1817, when he was eight, and in later life he had no distinct recollection of her beyond the 'black velvet gown'

she wore on her deathbed and her 'curiously constructed work-table' (*Autobiography*, 22). She was buried in St Chad's Church, Montford, near Shrewsbury, where Darwin's father also rests.

Childhood

Darwin's three older sisters took on maternal responsibility and he remembered his childhood with great affection. The nature of the relationship between father and son is disputed. Robert Waring Darwin was a talkative man of strong principles, freethinking, and an enthusiastic gardener. In later life Charles frequently referred to cherished medical and scientific opinions of his father, and he appreciated his father's powers of observation and intuitive understanding of human nature, qualities that enabled him to read 'the characters, and even the thoughts of those whom he saw even for a short time' (*Autobiography*, 32). Shrewd investments in canals and property made Dr Darwin prosperous, and through private mortgages and loans he kept a tight grip on the financial affairs of several Shrewsbury families. He was also a noted philanthropist. With a large medical practice and many friends, his life as a whig gentleman–physician

was comfortably full, varied, and respectable, even
if some nephews and nieces felt him to be dom-
ineering.

Charles Darwin's childhood is mainly known from
his own recollections, where he portrays himself
as a simple, docile, and happy child, with a liking
for long solitary walks. He showed an early habit
of fabricating adventures to seek attention. In 1817
he went to a day school run by George Case,
minister of the local Unitarian chapel, where his
mother (in keeping with her Wedgwood heritage)
had taken him to services. At Shrewsbury School,
which he attended as a boarder from 1818 to 1825,
the teaching was narrow and classical. Darwin
hated it and claimed that his daily facility in Latin
verse was forgotten by the next morning. Later
he recalled benefiting from little except private
lessons in Euclid, although he did enjoy reading
Shakespeare in private hours at school; at home he
dabbled in chemistry in a small laboratory fitted
up by his brother in an outhouse, but such science had no place in public schools, and when he
repeated experiments in the dormitories he was
publicly reproved by the headmaster, Dr Samuel
Butler, for wasting time. The boy was an inveterate collector, of franks, seals, coins, birds' eggs,

and minerals, and from early adolescence his passion became game shooting.

Edinburgh, 1825–1827

Robert Darwin intended both his sons to become physicians. Charles, unsuccessful at school, was removed in 1825, two years early, and spent the summer accompanying the doctor on his rounds. In the autumn he was sent with his brother Erasmus to Edinburgh University (1825–7), which offered the best medical education in Britain. Here English dissenters, barred from taking degrees at Oxford and Cambridge universities, kept abreast of continental work in the extramural schools and studied a suite of new sciences. The Darwins had studied medicine here for three generations, and Erasmus Darwin's grandsons found easy entrée to intellectual society. Leonard Horner took Charles to the Royal Society of Edinburgh, where he saw the novelist Sir Walter Scott. Diplomatic socializing with the professors, not least the elder Andrew Duncan, the octogenarian joint professor of the theory of physic (whose family vault contained the body of Darwin's uncle), preceded the term's work. However, after a diligent start,

Darwin recoiled at the early mornings: anatomy disgusted him, and his letters home criticized the professors. Civic politics had allowed some to treat their academic posts as family property, and he was appalled at the case of the anatomist Alexander Monro tertius—the third generation to hold the seat. While the younger Andrew Duncan's winter lectures on materia medica left Darwin with the enduring memory of spending 'a whole, cold, breakfastless hour on the properties of rhubarb' (*Correspondence*, 4.36), this probably said more about Darwin's youth and restlessness than about Duncan's abilities. Duncan was widely versed in European learning and at the forefront in teaching Augustin de Candolle's 'natural system' of classification (it was Candolle who emphasized the 'war' among species, so important to Darwin later). Most of all, Darwin was sickened by surgery (this was before the introduction of anaesthesia), and he fled during an operation on a child in the Royal Infirmary. All of this determined him to forsake the dead house and dissection, a decision he would later on occasion regret.

There were diversions: Thomas Hope's theatrical chemistry classes, coastal walks, and bird stuffing lessons, a craft taught to Darwin by a freed slave from Guiana, John Edmonstone, in the university natural history museum. After hiking through Wales during the summer of 1826, inspired by Gilbert White's *Natural History of Selborne* which taught him to see birds as more than targets, he returned to Edinburgh. His interest in medicine gone, he joined the thriving student Plinian Society. Here he heard the tyros talk on classification and cuckoos, and he even spoke himself. There was sometimes a frisson in these basement meetings in 1826, generated by a handful of young radical freethinkers using a deterministic science against the Church of Scotland. Darwin was nominated for the Plinian by the anti-clerical phrenologist William A. F. Browne, among others, and he petitioned to join on 21 November 1826, the day that Browne announced that he would refute Charles Bell's *Anatomy and Physiology of Expression* (which argued that the human facial muscles were specially created to express mankind's unique emotions). Darwin joined a week later, with the Unitarian W. R. Greg, who read a paper on lower animals' possessing every human mental faculty. Darwin himself was on the council of the Plinian Society by 5 December 1826.

Darwin's fascination for the local sea pens and sea mats on the Firth of Forth coast brought him briefly under the wing of his most influential mentor at Edinburgh, the physician and sponge expert Robert Edmond Grant, who guided Darwin's invertebrate studies in this rich North Sea environment. A Francophile and friend of Étienne Geoffroy Saint-Hilaire, Grant was a deist and materialist, and Darwin in old age recalled his bursting out with praise for the transformist Jean-Baptiste Lamarck. Indeed, Grant, like Lamarck, believed that the simple tissues of sponges and polyps could elucidate the primitive origin and primal function of complex human organs. Beneath Grant's stern crust Darwin found an enthusiast for this microscopic life, and Darwin made his own observations in March 1827 on the larvae of molluscs, the sea mat *Flustra*, and sea pens, confirming Grant's belief that sponge and sea-mat larvae could swim by means of cilia. Grant pushed Darwin into consulting continental books, including Lamarck's *System of Invertebrate Animals*, to check his *Flustra* findings. From late 1826 Grant took Darwin to meetings of the Wernerian Natural History Society, to which, on 24 March 1827, Grant announced Darwin's discovery that the black bodies inside oyster shells were the eggs of the skate leech *Pontobdella*. Three days later Darwin made his public début, presenting his findings on swimming *Flustra* larvae and *Pontobdella* eggs before the Plinian Society.

Darwin had read his grandfather Erasmus's book on the evolutionary laws of life and health, *Zoonomia*. Grant approved of it and exposed the grandson to the latest ideas on transmutation, endorsing Geoffroy's view that all animals showed a 'unity of plan'; from people to polyps, they shared similar organs that differed only in complexity. Thus life could be threaded into a chain, which for Grant represented a real blood line. His belief that the common origin of the plant and animal kingdoms lay just below the simplest algae and polyps, whose eggs were analogous to the 'monads', or elementary particles of living tissue, would provide a launch point for Darwin's own speculations a decade later. However, Grant's zoology was out of step with the safe taxonomic preoccupations of the age, and Darwin was exposed to the passions that such subversive science aroused. Browne's talk on the material basis of mind at the 27 March 1827 Plinian meeting so inflamed listeners that Darwin's début was probably overshadowed. Browne's propositions were struck out of the minute book in an act of censorship typical in the long tory years following the French Revolution (during which Darwin's own grandfather had been vilified). A sensitive eighteen-year old student could have been left in little doubt of the fate awaiting ideas that threatened to undermine spiritual and political authority.

Darwin remembered his Edinburgh years as a sterile period, but he was in rich scientific surroundings. He sat Robert Jameson's lectures in zoology and geology and heard Jameson explain rocks as sedimentary precipitates in opposition to Hope's view of granites as cooled crystals. Darwin, taking Hope's chemistry course, was teased to take his side in this old-fashioned debate. Jameson's course required Darwin to attend practical sessions three times a week in the magnificent museum, newly refurbished in 1826 and the fourth largest of its kind in Europe. Here budding civil engineers and East India Company men learned mineral types and colonial flora, while field trips taught them how to read strata sequences. This was an ideal training for a future imperial traveller.

Young and homesick, and loathing medicine, Darwin left Edinburgh in April 1827 without a degree. His father, a freethinker, fearing that he would become a wastrel on the family fortune, shrewdly decided on a clerical career. The complacent Church of England was ideal for an aimless son addicted to field sports, and once again Darwin followed his brother Erasmus, this time to Cambridge (where Erasmus had just finished his medical requirements) to read for the ordinary degree, the usual precursor to taking holy orders. His schoolboy Greek had to be revised, and he was tutored at home, not entering Christ's College until January 1828. Here Darwin found a cousin also preparing for the church, William Darwin Fox, who soon became his close friend. Though the idea of a comfortable parish appealed, Darwin had doubts about his faith, but he found nothing in Bishop John Pearson's *Exposition of the Creed* and the Revd John Bird Sumner's *Evidences of Christianity* that he could not believe.

The contrast between Edinburgh and Cambridge was total. Cambridge was a market town dominated by a medieval university, ruled by

clergymen and their proctors. Darwin avoided the
horsey set at Christ's and Fox introduced him to
beetle collecting in the local fens. For Darwin this
sport was compulsive and competitive. He identified his catches from standard texts, including
Lamarck's, and was thrilled to see his name in
print, in an instalment of J. F. Stephens's *Illustrations of British Entomology*. Expert advice was also
available at the Friday soirées held by the young
botany professor, the Revd John Stevens Henslow,
which were attended by other reverend professors, such as the geologist Adam Sedgwick and the
polymathic William Whewell. The dons' brilliant
conversation inspired Darwin to make a name for
himself in natural history; he attended Henslow's
botany course in 1829, and again in 1830 and 1831.

Formal studying became a desultory affair.
Darwin's mathematics suffered (as it always
would) and in the summer of 1828 he admitted
not feeling sufficiently inwardly moved by the
Holy Spirit to enter the church. His brother
Erasmus, already a freethinker, now lived in
London on the family purse, and when Fox left
Cambridge, Darwin latched on to Erasmus during
the vacations. Back in college he idled away his
time, ran up bills, drank, rode, and gambled.

There were greater temptations for the students. In spring 1829 the radicals Richard Carlile and the Revd Robert Taylor started an 'infidel home missionary tour' at Cambridge. They challenged the divines to a debate and sought converts before being hounded out of town. Taylor, a Cambridge graduate in holy orders, had been dubbed the Devil's Chaplain, and years later, as Darwin prepared to publish on evolution, he remembered the name and exclaimed 'What a book a Devil's chaplain might write on the ... horridly cruel works of nature!' (*Correspondence*, 6.178). He feared that he himself might be similarly reviled, an outcast from respectable society.

In March 1830 Darwin passed his first major exam, the 'little go', which included questions on the Revd William Paley's *Evidences of Christianity*, a book that Darwin relished. He became Henslow's walking companion, excelling himself on the professor's botany field trips and turning up early for lectures. Henslow's course was far removed from anything that Darwin had experienced at Edinburgh; it introduced him to plants as living organisms. Darwin employed his microscopical skills on plant fertilization processes, making good use of Henslow's knowledge of the recent work of French physiologists and the British botanist Robert Brown. Henslow taught Darwin about the properties of life and the dividing line between animals and plants. Darwin came to idolize his professor and said that their friendship was one of the most influential circumstances in his early life.

With Henslow as his tutor in 1830, Darwin studied mathematics and read Paley's *Principles of Moral and Political Philosophy* just as the agricultural unrest, or 'Swing riots', sweeping southern England reached Cambridge and 800 special constables were sworn in to protect the colleges. It was probably from this period that Darwin would remember how Henslow rejected Paley's utilitarian rationale for the established church. In the final BA examination in January 1831 Darwin ranked tenth in the pass-list of 178, surprising even himself. His residence requirement kept him in Cambridge, and he continued to seek Henslow's guidance. 'I do not know', Darwin confessed, 'whether I love or respect' him more (*Correspondence*, 1.123). He read the last of Paley's trilogy, the *Natural Theology*, with its argument for a designer God from the adaptation of living species to their environments. This was the cornerstone of Cambridge science, along with John Herschel's *Preliminary Discourse on the Study of Natural Philosophy*, which inspired Darwin further in his scientific career. After reading Alexander von Humboldt's *Personal Narrative* of his voyage to the tropics, Darwin began planning a month's expedition with friends to Tenerife. In preparation he attended Sedgwick's geology lectures in spring 1831 and in August accompanied Sedgwick (at Henslow's request) to north Wales for two weeks in the field. It was the best possible training, much more effective than the dry lectures at Edinburgh, which had made Darwin vow never to 'attend to Geology' (*Autobiography*, 53). Sedgwick built up Darwin's expertise and self-confidence, introducing him to some of the most perplexing geological issues of the day. Then, on returning to Shrewsbury, Darwin found a letter from Henslow offering him passage on a ship headed round the world.

The *Beagle* voyage, 1831–1836

Darwin joins the captain

Henslow's letter referred to a proposed two-year trip to 'Terra del Fuego & home by the East Indies', explaining that the position was 'more as a companion than a mere collector'. Henslow had recommended Darwin, 'not on the supposition of yr. being a finished Naturalist, but as amply qualified for collecting, observing, & noting any thing worthy to be noted in Natural History' (*Correspondence*, 1.128–9). This was not an official vacancy open to all. It was a private arrangement originating with the captain, Robert FitzRoy, a nephew of the duke of Grafton, who asked Francis Beaufort, hydrographer to the navy, to find a well-educated gentleman with scientific interests who could make good use of such a voyage. The search thus made its way through a network of Cambridge professors and their Admiralty friends, via Henslow and his brother-in-law, the Revd Leonard Jenyns (both of whom would have accepted but for family commitments), and on to Darwin. At first Darwin's father objected so strongly that Darwin felt obliged to refuse, but his uncle Josiah Wedgwood was in favour and Dr Darwin relented. Afterwards he provided every assistance, including the cost of equipping his son and covering all of his considerable expenses during the voyage.

On 1 September 1831 Darwin accepted and went to Cambridge to consult Henslow. In London he met FitzRoy and was approved by him. Darwin was also taken with the captain. The *Beagle* had recently returned from South America after a two-ship expedition (1827–30) commanded by Phillip Parker King, which had surveyed a large part of the eastern coast, a region significant in naval and commercial terms for Great Britain during Canning's ministry. On that voyage FitzRoy had assumed temporary command of the *Beagle* after the suicide of Captain Pringle Stokes. FitzRoy was appointed overall commander for a second voyage to complete the survey. Darwin now prepared himself, visiting naturalists at the British Museum and Zoological Society, learning preserving techniques, getting his equipment in order, and visiting the *Beagle*, under refit at the naval base of Devonport in Plymouth. He sought advice from Robert Brown about travelling microscopes and worried about the lack of room on board. The *Beagle* was a converted 10-gun brig, only 90 feet long, capacity 242 tons, popularly known as one of the 'coffin' class. Arriving at Devonport in October, Darwin found that departure was delayed. He grew anxious, with heart pains, and feared that he might have to abandon the voyage. When the ship did sail, it was forced to return to port twice because of storms. The *Beagle* left finally on 27 December 1831, by which time much of Darwin's initial excitement had disappeared.

On board the *Beagle*

The voyage, which lasted five years, was the key formative event in Darwin's life. It 'determined my whole career' (*Autobiography*, 76), giving him an unrivalled opportunity to make observations, collect animals and plants, and explore some of the most beautiful, desolate, and isolated places in the world. Under FitzRoy the voyage's objectives extended to include geophysical measurements, and the *Beagle* was equipped with a variety of instruments and devices, including a lightning conductor and a large number of marine chronometers for measuring longitude. The Admiralty intended the officers to make a chain of exceptionally accurate measurements round the globe. The ship also carried out trials on Beaufort's wind scale. Supernumeraries in FitzRoy's private employment were appointed, including an artist, Augustus Earle (replaced *en route* by Conrad Martens in 1833), and an instrument-tender, George Stebbing. The voyage was also to be more of a Christianizing and civilizing mission than most imperial cruises: a novice missionary, Richard Matthews, was on board, accompanied by three native Fuegians who had been taken hostage by FitzRoy on the previous voyage, carried to England, and briefly educated with a view to establishing an Anglican mission in Tierra del Fuego. Darwin was independently financed but on the Admiralty books for victuals. He was the only member of the ship who held any intimacy with the captain; they usually dined together, and they shared a number of adventures. FitzRoy at times seemed as unstable as his uncle Lord Castlereagh, who had committed suicide, and he and Darwin occasionally argued, once in Plymouth and again in Brazil, over slavery (which Darwin abhorred), when Darwin nearly left the ship. But FitzRoy wanted Darwin aboard, not least perhaps to allay his own fears about mental instability and spare him Pringle Stokes's fate. Although the young tory aristocrat and Darwin became friends, even publishing a short paper on missionary activity together in 1836, their views and temperaments were at root incompatible, and afterwards they drifted apart.

Darwin slept and worked in the poop cabin, which he shared with the mate and draughtsman, John Lort Stokes, and midshipman Philip Gidley King, son of the former commander. He befriended the officers, especially the second lieutenant, Bartholomew Sulivan, and one or another often joined him in his natural history ventures. In 1833 FitzRoy gave Darwin permission to employ as a personal assistant one of the cabin boys, Syms Covington (who would remain with him afterwards until 1839). Darwin's collecting activities amused the sailors and earned him the nickname Philos, meaning ship's philosopher.

The *Beagle* visited the Cape Verde Islands (January 1832), Brazil (April–July 1832), Montevideo and Buenos Aires (July–November 1832), Tierra del Fuego and Cape Horn (December 1832–January 1833, February 1834), the Falkland Islands (March–April 1833, March–April 1834), Patagonia (April 1833–January 1834), the west coast of South America (Chiloé, Valparaiso, Lima: June 1834–July 1835), the Galápagos Islands (September–October 1835), Tahiti (November 1835), New Zealand (December 1835), Australia (Sydney, January 1836; Tasmania, February; King George's Sound, March), the Cocos (Keeling) Islands (April 1836), Mauritius (April–May 1836), Cape Town (May–June 1836), and St Helena and Ascension (July 1836). Darwin participated in all the excitements of the voyage. He joined the carnival in Brazil, witnessed revolutions in Montevideo and Lima, and saw gauchos exterminating the natives on the pampas. He watched Mount Osorno erupting on 26 November 1834 while on the island of Chiloé and experienced an earthquake in the woods outside Valdivia. He walked through the ruins of the town of Concepción, destroyed by the same earthquake, on 20 February 1835, and declared them to be 'the most awful yet interesting spectacle I ever beheld' (*Diary*, ed. Keynes, 296). It was a humbling vision that revealed the powerlessness of people and impermanence of their works before the awesome forces of nature. He proved a stalwart member of inland expeditions and a good shot, often helping to supply fresh meat for the crew. After a dangerous escape from an enormous wave created by a calving glacier, when Darwin's quick action saved lives, FitzRoy named an expanse of water and a mountain in the Beagle Channel in his honour. His shipmates all warmly vouched for his even humour, resilience, and likeable manners, and he similarly remembered them with affection. The only exception was the ship's surgeon, Robert McCormick, who left the voyage at Rio de Janeiro in 1832, apparently annoyed at the preference given to Darwin's collecting over his own. The privileges of a self-financed captain's companion showed too in the invitations Darwin received to join polite society ashore.

Expeditions and collections

Playing no part in the ship's daily orders, Darwin often travelled overland. In Patagonia he made several expeditions, riding over 70 miles from Maldonado in May 1833, from Patagones to Bahia Blanca that August, and in September–October 1833 he rode 700 miles from Bahia Blanca, via

Buenos Aires, to Santa Fe. In November he set off again, from Montevideo to Mercedes, to see the Rio Uruguay. On the west coast he rode to the base of the Andes in August–September 1834, and in March–April 1835 trekked across the cordilleras, from Valparaiso through the Portillo Pass to Mendoza. On another occasion he was seriously ill with a fever, brought on, he thought, by sour wine, and recuperated for five weeks in the house of an old school friend, Richard Corfield, who lived in Valparaiso. Always he studied the local geology and natural history, whether travelling or more permanently based in lodgings. For three months in 1832 he rented a cottage on Botofogo Bay near Rio de Janeiro, where he hunted, dredged, and collected corallines and plants. The pleasure he took in tropical vegetation and alpine scenery was both aesthetic and scientific. It fuelled his growing sense of purpose as a naturalist.

Darwin's geological achievements mounted up. Using Charles Lyell's radical new *Principles of Geology* (1830–33) as a guide, he grew bold in interpreting the earth's crust by causes now in operation. (The first volume was a gift from FitzRoy, the other two reached him during the voyage.) He was captivated by Lyell's grand theoretical scheme—'when seeing a thing never seen by Lyell, one yet saw it partially through his eyes' (*Correspondence*, 3.55)—and confirmed many of Lyell's observations with careful field-work. On other points Darwin expanded innovatively, especially in understanding the piecemeal formation of the Andes and the origin of coral reefs on sinking mountain rims. There was an immediacy to it all. After experiencing the Concepción earthquake in 1835, Darwin found the shoreline raised a few feet and mussel beds lifted out of the sea, confirming his Lyellian incremental upthrust theory. As he trekked through the Portillo and Uspallata passes of the Andes, the coloured rocks seemed almost like a geological diagram, and in the Cocos (Keeling) Islands he waded over the reefs to confirm his theory of the formation of coral atolls. His geology was dynamic, with continents slowly rising and sea basins sinking, and it formed the basis of all his later views. He endorsed Lyell's belief in an earth gradually shaped over countless ages: time enough—as he later grasped—for evolution by natural selection to occur.

Darwin's collections were extensive. At Punta Alta near Bahia Blanca he found fossilized remains of gigantic extinct mammals, which at the time he thought must belong to mastodons, armadillos, and megatheriums (ground sloths). The fossils were later identified as belonging to previously unknown giant species. The cause of their extinction puzzled him because the remains were embedded with species of shells still in existence. In the far south of Patagonia he collected a new species of rhea (well known to local inhabitants), which he afterwards used to illustrate the geographical differentiation of species. He collected a great number of insects, birds, molluscs, small vertebrates, invertebrates, and plants, recording their provenance, living appearance, and behaviour in field notebooks and diaries. Crates of specimens were periodically shipped back to Henslow for storage. Henslow encouraged William Buckland and William Clift to exhibit some of the megatherium remains at the Cambridge meeting of the British Association for the Advancement of Science in 1833, and in 1835 Henslow published extracts on natural history topics from Darwin's letters. These were read at meetings of the Cambridge Philosophical Society and the Geological Society of London.

Ironically, what proved to be the most famous collection of all, the birds from the Galápagos

Islands, was carelessly labelled. Darwin did not notice the diversification of finch species on separate islands during the *Beagle*'s five-week visit, although the English resident on Charles Island informed him that the giant tortoises were island-specific, and Darwin realized that the mocking-birds were too. Thus, identifying the finch skins proved difficult when he returned to London. Even so, the Galápagos Islands impressed him greatly. He was fascinated by the iguanas, giant tortoises, mockingbirds, and other birds, as well as the volcanic geology. The relations between the species on different islands, and between the island species and those of continental South America, were, however, sufficiently puzzling for him to allude to them in his ornithological notes on the return voyage. He seems to have wondered about the possibility of transmutation at this time.

Darwin was stirred by the diverse human populations he met, ranging from expatriate Europeans to indigenous tribes. His writings contain colourful references to gauchos, with whom he travelled across Argentina, the Patagonian 'Indians', Tahitians, Maori, and Australian Aborigines, as well as missionaries, colonists, slaves, and emigré Cornish miners. He met General

Rosas (leading the war to exterminate the native Patagonians) in August 1833 and was caught up in military blockades. The most unsettling of all Darwin's encounters was with the native inhabitants of Tierra del Fuego. He was stunned by their naked 'savage' state, particularly in comparison with the three fine-clothed Fuegians on board. 'I would not have believed how entire the difference between savage & civilized man is.— It is greater than between a wild & domesticated animal' (*Diary*, ed. Keynes, 122). Yet the fact that Fuegians could be 'civilized' (as Darwin saw it) confirmed his belief that, under the skin, humans were all one species, and this remained a lasting influence on his later evolutionary theories. During the *Beagle*'s time in the far south Darwin and FitzRoy were sad to note that the three Anglicized Fuegians soon returned to the aboriginal state.

Darwin suffered from sea-sickness throughout, and his longing for home grew with his maturity as a naturalist. As the voyage ended, his love of nature was ousting the church: 'your situation is above envy', he wrote to his clerical cousin Fox; 'to a person fit to take the office, the life of a Clergyman is a type of all that is respectable &

happy' (*Correspondence*, 1.460). But Darwin himself now had other plans. The voyage had fostered an intellectual ferment and fortified him to re-evaluate all of natural history. His future, he believed, lay in the élite world of London science. He disembarked at Falmouth on 2 October 1836 and arrived at Shrewsbury two days later, where his sister Caroline realized that he had gained an 'interest for the rest of his life' (ibid., 1.505).

Theorizing in London, 1836–1842

Recording the voyage

After visiting Cambridge to consult Henslow about experts to describe his *Beagle* specimens, and calling on his Wedgwood relatives in Staffordshire, Darwin stayed with his brother in London for a few weeks. During the five-year voyage the whigs had established a new workhouse regime for the losers in a Malthusian competitive economy. Erasmus Darwin was intimate with the poor-law propagandist Harriet Martineau, which put him at the heart of the whig machine, and Darwin's cousin Hensleigh Wedgwood, whose wedding to Frances Mackintosh had been attended by Thomas Robert Malthus's daughter as a bridesmaid, completed the two brothers' dining circle. The landlubber had moved straight into an aggressively Malthusian, reforming environment.

On 29 October 1836 Darwin first met the geologist Charles Lyell in person. They became close friends, and Lyell introduced him to the comparative anatomist Richard Owen. In December and January 1837 Owen received Darwin's pampas fossils at the Royal College of Surgeons; Thomas Bell accepted the *Beagle* reptiles, Leonard Jenyns the fish, George Robert Waterhouse the mammals, and John Gould the birds. After obtaining a £1000 Treasury grant through Henslow's government contacts, Darwin arranged for the naturalists' technical descriptions to be published in nineteen numbers as *The Zoology of the Voyage of H.M.S. Beagle* (1838–43; reissued in five parts, 1839–43). The plants and insects, which Darwin planned to include, and the marine invertebrates that he intended to tackle himself, were described piecemeal in other publications. Henslow, to whom Darwin gave the plants, later sent them to Joseph Dalton Hooker for identification.

Darwin lived in Cambridge until March 1837, working on his manuscripts and specimens, and lecturing at the Cambridge Philosophical Society on the lightning-fused glass tubes in the Maldonado sand dunes. On 4 January he read his first scientific paper, 'Observations of proofs of recent elevation on the coast of Chile', as a new fellow of the Geological Society of London. Lyell's influence showed in Darwin's discussion of the slowly rising Chilean coastline, compensated by a sinking Pacific, but some of his views were un-Lyellian, notably that coral reefs crowned mountains disappearing under sea. Darwin soon established himself as a gentleman geologist, at one with the urban gentry and clerical dons: he became a council member of the Geological Society in 1837 and a secretary in 1838. He was also vice-president of the Entomological Society in 1838.

Living on £400 a year from his father, Darwin enjoyed independence. He turned his *Beagle* diary into a book of travels. It was finished by June 1837 and published in May 1839 as *Journal and Remarks, 1832–1836*, the third volume of FitzRoy's *Narrative of the Surveying Voyages*, and again separately on 15 August 1839 as *Journal of researches into the geology and natural history of the various countries visited by H.M.S. Beagle under the command of Captain FitzRoy, R. N., from 1832–1836*. Meanwhile Darwin continued sorting the *Beagle* collections for distribution to specialists and sometimes bought in expert help, such as that of the engraver George Sowerby. Bit by bit, his collections ended up in major scientific institutions.

The expert reports on his collections surprised him. Darwin had initially thought that his pampas fossils were huge extinct forms allied to rhinoceroses and mastodons (both found on other continents), as well as megatheriums, but Owen diagnosed a capybara relative, *Toxodon*, an anteater-like *Scelidotherium*, ground sloth *Mylodon*, armadillo *Glyptodon*, and llama-like *Macrauchenia*. These identifications suggested that some 'law of succession' had caused the previous South American mammals to be replaced by others of their own kind. On 4 January 1837 Darwin presented the Zoological Society museum with eighty preserved mammals and 450 birds. Within days Gould discovered that the Galápagos birds, misunderstood by Darwin as a mixture of finches, wrens, 'Gross-beaks', and blackbird-relatives, were in fact a closely related (and new) group of differentially adapted ground finches. Gould also distinguished the small rhea that Darwin had collected as a new species, *Rhea darwinii* (subsequently renamed).

Transmutation

On 6 March 1837 Darwin moved from Cambridge to London lodgings, at 36 Great Marlborough Street, close to his brother. Here the secular milieu was more conducive to his private musings on extinction and repopulation arising from Owen's, Gould's, and his own geological findings. In Erasmus's freethinking circle Martineau believed in the natural predetermination of human life and Wedgwood interested himself in the genealogy of languages (itself a sort of evolution). Darwin attended soirées hosted by the mathematician Charles Babbage. Babbage's in-press *Ninth Bridgewater Treatise* made God a legislator, working pre-eminently through grand laws rather than miracles. This was the rational whig answer to what John Herschel had called the 'mystery of mysteries' (Cannon, 'Impact'), the cause of the replacement of species through time. By early 1837 Darwin too accepted that 'the Creator creates by ... laws' (Barrett and others, *Notebooks*, B98).

In March that year Gould recognized Darwin's four Galápagos mockingbirds (which, unlike the finches, Darwin had labelled by island) as three separate species. The island-specific types suggested to Darwin that they were mainland South American castaways that had changed to meet local conditions. Darwin belatedly examined FitzRoy's labelled finches to confirm that each too was island-specific. Bell's work on the giant Galápagos tortoises and Waterhouse's on the rodents further confirmed that representative species were the rule on these islands.

Inured, perhaps, to transmutation by the works of his grandfather Erasmus and Grant, Darwin came to accept the idea unquestioningly early in 1837, even though 'evolution' (an anachronistic word, 'descent' he called it from 1838) was detested by his Cambridge mentors and assailed in Lyell's *Principles of Geology*. This was a year and a half before he devised a definite causal mechanism. Owen, preparing his first Hunterian lectures at the College of Surgeons, stimulated Darwin's search for the laws of living matter. Unlike Henslow, who had taught that the matter inside pollen granules was inert, and that life was impressed from without, Owen accepted that the embryonic germ had an intrinsic 'organizing energy' that directed its development and waned as the tissues grew. Darwin would stretch this 'organizing energy' to transmutational (and to Owen illicit) lengths. Like Grant's radical anatomists, Darwin in his most radical phase (1837 to mid-1838) considered living atoms to be self-organizing. He now returned to the intense questioning monologues started in his 'red' notebook during the last months of the *Beagle* voyage. Were extinctions due to species senescence? If island isolation on the Galápagos was necessary for species formation (to stop back-blending with mainland parents), how to explain the overlapping ranges of the two species of Patagonian rhea? Were changes produced *per saltum*, with no blending intermediates? Were new species 'monsters' from the womb, of the sort then being mooted by Owen?

In July 1837 Darwin opened his first notebook on transmutation, which he labelled 'B' (his 'A' notebook was mostly concerned with geology). Thus began two years of secret telegraphic jottings on the mechanics of organic change. He first toyed with Lamarck's and Grant's idea of the spontaneous generation of monads driving the escalator of life 'upwards', and his joke, 'If all men were dead then monkeys make men.— Men make angels' (Barrett and others, *Notebooks*,

B169), showed his defiance of clerical fears of a simian ancestry. Then his thoughts became relativistic, radically departing from Lamarck's. He foreswore any unidirectional change; life merely adapted to local habitats. He developed a non-human orientation and found it 'absurd to talk of one animal being higher than another', for humans and bees would have different criteria of 'highness' (ibid., B74). He conceived life rather as a branching tree, and he jettisoned a continuous spontaneous generation of life in favour of a single Precambrian emergence. He rejected, too, his own former idea of species senescence, which would cause all the creatures on a branch to die out together. A species died out, he now thought, because conditions changed too fast.

Faltering health accompanied these disturbing conclusions. Darwin now led a double life, mixing with the Oxford and Cambridge divines at the respectable Geological Society while secretly plumbing a materialistic transmutation. He read papers to the Geological on the pampas fossils and coral reefs in May 1837, on the formation of mould through the action of worms in November, and on the earthquake and volcanic causes of Andean uplift in March 1838. The worms, corals, and incremental uplift expressed his belief in small causes producing large results, as would come to be the case in his secret evolutionary views. Behind this façade his contempt for the anthropocentric divines grew. He privately scoffed at the Geological Society's president, William Whewell, who 'says length of days adapted to duration of sleep of man!!! whole universe so adapted!!! ... instance of arrogance!!' (Barrett and others, *Notebooks*, D49). Darwin's acceptance by the geological élite, which decried materialistic science as morally corrupting and politically seditious, only accentuated his double life.

As the tory–Anglicans were ousted from town halls in countrywide reforms, Darwin was evicting their providential God from a reformed biology. Of Unitarian stock himself, he expressed radical dissenting sentiments in his notebooks, sentiments of equality, anti-slavery, and anti-privilege to sustain a levelling kinship with all life: 'Animals—whom we have made our slaves we do not like to consider our equals.—Do not slave holders wish to make the black man other kind?' (Barrett and others, *Notebooks*, B231). He also saw pain run through the whole creation: 'animals our fellow brethren in pain, disease death &

suffering ... they may partake, from our origin
in one common ancestor we may all be netted
together' (ibid., B232). But whatever his sanc-
tion from dissenting political gains in the country,
he knew that his speculations would alienate the
Anglican establishment, which saw evolution as
a threat to belief in human accountability in the
next world and with it their paternalistic control
of this one.

In 1838 Darwin filled three notebooks ('C', 'D',
and 'E') on transmutation, and parallel 'M' and
'N' notebooks on the behavioural, psychological,
and metaphysical implications of evolution for
mankind. Evolution from the first was designed
to explain human morality no less than body
form. Darwin's first sight of an ape, an orang-
utan, at London Zoo, on 28 March 1838, led
him to make notes on her human-like emotions.
He began studying the expressions and behaviour of monkeys. More and more a cultural and
genetic determinist (dismissing free will at this
time), he accepted that morality was culture-
relative and saw its origin in the social instincts
of troop animals. To Plato's claim that 'our "necessary ideas [of good and evil]" arise from the
preexistence of the soul', Darwin responded, 'read

monkeys for preexistence' (Barrett and others, *Notebooks*, M128). Other remarks left no doubt that he grasped the implications, such as 'whole [miraculous] fabric totters & falls' (ibid., C76).

Darwin explained the inheritance of instincts by means of their coding in the nervous system, and considered even the 'love of deity [an] effect of organization. oh you Materialist!' (Barrett and others, *Notebooks*, C166). In an age when science was expected to underpin traditional values, such materialism, had it been made public, would have been anathema to conservatives. Darwin, an anomalous theorizer in an age primarily concerned with describing and classifying, was not about to expose himself. His rising career—he was elected to the Athenaeum Club in 1838, the Royal Society of London in 1839, and the council of the Royal Geographical Society in 1840—served to emphasize how much he stood to lose. He had seen the Plinian Society censorship and was familiar with the anatomist William Lawrence's disgrace for holding materialist ideas. On one occasion Darwin had a nightmare of execution, which he recorded in his notebook, and he began conceiving disarming tactics: 'Mention persecution of early Astronomers' (ibid., C123).

Overwork and ill health drove Darwin to the Scottish highlands in summer 1838, where he visited the parallel 'roads' of Glen Roy. These he compared to the terraced beaches in Chile, in accordance with his theory of rising mountains and sinking sea basins. The roads were the subject of his 1839 'Observations on the parallel roads of Glen Roy', published in the *Philosophical Transactions of the Royal Society*. He would later characterize the paper as 'one long gigantic blunder' (*Correspondence*, 9.255) because it had taken no account of the effects of glaciation. Of no other part of his life's work was he ever so frankly self-critical.

Marriage and Malthus

Early in 1838 Darwin's thoughts turned to marriage. By now an inveterate cataloguer, he drew up a cost-benefit analysis (*Correspondence*, 1.443–5). To his mind, the advantages materially outweighed the disadvantages and he became engaged to his first cousin Emma Wedgwood (1808–1896) a few months later, almost routinely. She considered him the most 'transparent man I ever saw' (*Emma Darwin*, 2.6) and, going against his father's advice, Darwin confided to her his secret beliefs. Probably she was shocked, for while visiting her at her home in Maer, Staffordshire, Darwin noted that he must disguise 'stating how far, I believe, in Materialism' (Barrett and others, *Notebooks*, M57). Nevertheless, the two became warmly devoted to each other. About that time he also sensed the importance of his work. In the summer of 1838 he began recording the events of his life in a journal, starting with a 1700-word recollection of his childhood (this also formed part of his research into the nature of mind and memory). Emma was devout, an Anglican by baptism, with Unitarian convictions, and although her fears for Charles's eternal salvation became a sad undercurrent during the early years of the marriage, she remained steadily sympathetic and supportive towards her husband.

In September 1838 Darwin studied books on human statistics. With distress rising round him and the workhouses going up, Malthus was highly topical; Darwin read his *Essay on the Principle of Population*. From it he quickly came to appreciate that overpopulation must be the factor driving competition and selection, for:

being well prepared to appreciate the struggle for existence ... it at once struck me that

under these circumstances favourable variations would tend to be preserved, and
unfavourable ones to be destroyed. Here, then,
I had at last got a theory by which to work.
(*Autobiography*, 120)

Malthus's doctrine that human population tends
to double every twenty-five years (if there is no
check or restriction) struck Darwin in his primed
state, even as he planned to marry and repro-
duce. The numbers of animals and plants were
not stable, as he had thought; too many individuals were born, in nature as in society. Competition left only the best adapted, those most able
to leave offspring. Each stage in the genealogical
ascent was 'the surviving one of ten thousand
trials' (Barrett and others, *Notebooks*, Mac58*v*);
millions must die so that the species remained
fitted to changing conditions. Darwin recorded
this new insight in his 'D' notebook in an entry
dated 28 September. With its kernel of Malthusian overpopulation and struggle, Darwin's private view synchronized with the social theories
of the whig grandees and was divorced from
those of the anti-Malthusian radicals. But even
though William Paley's happy nature gave way
to Malthus's bleaker image, Darwin, retaining his

creedless rational faith, still saw 'descent' as God's mechanism for this 'production of higher animals' (ibid., OUN37).

Darwin's faith was too slim even for Emma. She took him to King's College Church, London, but he had ceased to believe in divine revelation. With £10,000 from Dr Darwin and Emma's dowry of £5000, plus an allowance of £400 a year, the couple were wealthy. Married by a cousin, the Revd John Allen Wedgwood, on 29 January 1839 at St Peter's Church, Maer, they moved into a rented house in Upper Gower Street, London, where Emma soon became pregnant.

By now Darwin accepted that mental as well as bodily variations arose by chance. Selection worked on randomly altering instincts. It became irrelevant whether or not instincts were coded in the brain, and this allowed Darwin to play down his mental materialism, with its over-tones of atheistic radicalism. However, the ran-domness of Darwin's new nature made it even more irreconcilable to a higher design, although he still portrayed nature anthropomorphically as a sort of omnipotent breeder who selected the most useful traits. Having grown up among the agricultural gentry, he studied livestock husbandry as a matter of course. He discussed fancy breeds, particularly dogs, with William Yarrell and learned how breeders picked the desired traits from each litter; he talked with agriculturists and gardeners at every opportunity. Although Darwin opened a 'Questions and experiments' notebook in 1839 on husbandry issues and sent country gentlemen of his acquaintance a list of 'Questions about the breeding of animals', the analogy between natural and artificial selection that was to underpin all his subsequent work was already complete. On 10 July 1839 Darwin closed his 'E' notebook—his last major transmutation notebook.

The Darwins began to withdraw, giving up parties and the old circles. The man who saw contingency rule biology led a routine life, his days alike 'as two peas' (*Correspondence*, 2.236). Stomach troubles, flatulence, and nausea began to plague him, marking the onset of the illness that would dog his life. But he was delighted by the birth of their first child, William Erasmus (1839–1914), on 27 December 1839. The child's expressions fascinated Darwin, who took notes comparing them to those of animals. An extended period of vomiting in 1840 forced Darwin to reduce his workload and seek medical help from a distant cousin, the society physician Henry Holland. He spent two summers seriously ill, cared for by his wife at her family home. Back in London he shunned unnecessary contacts and resigned as secretary of the Geological Society in 1841. When his paper on the distribution of the erratic boulders and their transport by ice-floes in South America was finished, he asked Hensleigh Wedgwood to read it to the society, delegating in a way that was to increase over the years.

The couple's second child, Anne Elizabeth (1841–1851), was born on 2 March 1841. Darwin finished his *Structure and Distribution of Coral Reefs* (1842), the first volume in a trilogy on the geology of South America, and studied humble-bees boring through the corollas of flowers (publishing a note in the *Gardeners' Chronicle*). His theoretical isolation was soon accompanied by the physical: he persuaded his father to lend him the money to buy a rural retreat in Down, Kent. Before moving he wrote a 35-page sketch of his evolution theory, completed in June 1842, which enumerated the arguments for descent and his Malthusian mechanism of natural selection but skirted the origin of morality and the ancestry of mankind. He had no intention of publishing immediately, certainly not that summer, with industrial Britain riot-torn and suffering a general strike.

Parish naturalist, 1842–1856

Retreat to Down

In September 1842 Darwin moved the family to Down, a parish of about 400 inhabitants on the North Downs, 16 miles from London. Here, at 'the extreme verge of the world' (*Correspondence*, 2.352), he found security in an old parsonage with 15 acres of land. Down House would be his refuge for the next forty years. Much of his life here resembled that of a prosperous country parson, the sort of man he had once intended to be.

Finding that going to London 'so generally knocks me up, that I am able to do scarcely anything' (*Correspondence*, 2.355), he increasingly dropped out of metropolitan society. He undertook his major works at home, fitting out his estate as a place for natural history researches of a gentlemanly kind. He had the house renovated and extended, the lawns landscaped, gardens dug, and the road outside his study window lowered to keep passers-by from peering inside. A grove of trees was planted where he laid out his thinking path, the 'Sandwalk', and he began (but abandoned) a country diary, following in the footsteps of the Revd Gilbert White. Over the winter of 1843–4, with the second volume of his *Beagle* geology, *Volcanic Islands*, going into print, Darwin transformed the pencil sketch of his species theory into a coherent essay. He broached the subject of transmutation with a few friends with trepidation, fearing that his ideas would appear as 'the merest trash'. 'I am almost convinced (quite contrary to the opinion I started with) that species are not (it is like confessing a murder) immutable', he wrote to the young Kew botanist Joseph Dalton Hooker: 'You will groan, & think to yourself "on what a man have I been wasting my time..."' (ibid., 3.2). Hooker, however, was not put off. Buoyed by his response, Darwin finished the 231-page manuscript in February 1844. He had it copied out neatly by a local schoolmaster and entrusted it to his wife with a letter to be opened in the event of his 'sudden death', stating as his 'most solemn & last request' that she should engage an editor to publish his theory posthumously. 'If it be accepted even by one competent judge, it will be a considerable step in science' (ibid., 3.43).

Darwin's motives for not publishing at this point undoubtedly involved prudence mixed with great anxiety. His *Journal* had given him an entrée into scientific society worldwide and a reputation among travellers; animals and plants were now named after him; among London's savants he was also rated highly—he served as a Geological Society vice-president in 1844; and, not least, there were his clerical friends, determined to keep science responsible and supporting the creationist *status quo*: an ill-spoken word and Darwin's reputation would be in peril. Indeed, he watched as a popularization of evolution, *Vestiges of the Natural History of Creation* (1844), shocked intellectual society only weeks after he finished his essay. He read the reviews uneasily, knowing that the anonymous book—by the publisher Robert Chambers—had even been attributed to him, 'at which', he admitted, 'I ought to be much flattered & unflattered' (*Correspondence*, 3.181). *Vestiges* attracted considerable scientific and theological abuse, particularly from conservatives. Darwin would not expose his own theory and risk enduring the same fate, but at the same time he felt driven to amass more and more authoritative evidence to support it.

Hooker, though sceptical of transmutation, became Darwin's sounding board and sparring partner, a trusted friend whose encyclopaedic knowledge of plants was constantly at his disposal. It was Hooker who inadvertently goaded him into his next project by remarking that only one who had studied many species was qualified to discuss their origin. Thus after finishing his last book based on the *Beagle* voyage, *Geological Observations on South America* (1846), Darwin turned to barnacles. He intended only to describe an anomalous tiny species he had brought back from southern Chile, *Arthrobalanus*, but ended up dissecting and describing all known species, living and extinct. What he found confirmed his ideas about the origin of the sexes from hermaphrodite invertebrate ancestors and strengthened his belief in transmutation. Every part of every species was variable, and he worked out how barnacles had descended from their crab-like relatives.

Illness and family life

During this period the family grew and prospered. Emma, constantly pregnant for the first twelve years of marriage, bore eight more children: Mary Eleanor, who died three weeks old in 1842; Henrietta Emma (1843–1929), George Howard (1845–1912), Elizabeth (1847–1926), Francis (1848–1925), Leonard (1850–1943), Horace (1851–1928), and Charles Waring (1856–1858). With his father's help Darwin planned carefully for their future, acquiring land in Lincolnshire and reinvesting the income from his and Emma's portfolios. Prosperous respectability would be the children's legacy. Following his friend J. S. Henslow's example Darwin became a pillar of the parish. He subscribed towards church improvements and advised the incumbent, the Revd John Innes, on educational and charitable matters. Darwin became treasurer of the village Coal and Clothing Club, and in 1850 he and Innes founded the Down Friendly Society, with Darwin serving as guardian and treasurer. He also discussed charitable and village business with Sir John Lubbock, the mathematician and banker, whose house, High Elms, was nearby.

Darwin's stomach continued to plague him. He experimented on himself, giving up snuff and trying faddish electrotherapies, to no avail. His father, whom he revered, was a constant source of medical advice. After his death in 1848, Darwin's health deteriorated sharply, with vomiting fits, flatulence, fainting sensations, and black spots before his eyes, and he again placed himself in the hands of Dr Holland. He grew despondent, expecting his own imminent death, and was tortured by anxiety. He had even been too ill, he said, to reach Shrewsbury in time for his father's funeral (although he had arrived later in the day). With Emma's support, he turned to religious literature, but by now he was unable to believe 'in the same spirit... that ladies do believe on all & every subject' (*Correspondence*, 3.141). Just after his fortieth birthday in 1849 he fled in desperation for four months—his longest absence from Down—to a water-cure establishment at Malvern run by the fashionable hydropathist James Manby Gully. The water cure seemed to work and Darwin kept up the energetic cold-water regime when he returned home, with Joseph Parslow, the Down House butler, sluicing him down. He shivered with cold, plodding to and from a specially built outside shower-house throughout the winter. Darwin varied the treatment according to Gully's instructions and recorded his daily symptoms obsessively, and elliptically, for six years in a foolscap health diary. After many relapses, and fearing that his ailment was a heritable defect, he gave up 'all hopes of ever being a strong man again' (ibid., 4.369).

In 1850 Anne, his eldest daughter and favourite, became ill. Just before Easter 1851 Darwin took her to Malvern, confident of Gully's care, but here she developed a virulent fever and died. Emma, pregnant, stayed at Down, praying in vain. Afterwards neither of them could 'see on any side a gleam of comfort' (*Correspondence*, 5.27). Darwin himself found no consolation in Christianity for what he called 'our bitter & cruel loss' (ibid., 5.32). He composed a moving threnody, portraying 'Annie' as an example of human nature in its physical and moral perfection. 'Formed to live a life of happiness' (ibid., 5.542), she had fallen in the amoral struggle for existence, and Darwin now came to believe that all of his children had inherited his poor constitution. 'My dread is hereditary ill-health. Even death is better for them' (ibid., 5.84).

The Darwins were wealthy from his £50,000 inheritance, interest on mortgages, and rent from Lincolnshire farms at Beesby and Sutterton Fen (bequeathed by his father). There was also Emma's £25,000 trust fund, and her interest in the Wedgwood firm inherited on her father's death in 1843. By investing in the Leeds and Bradford Railway, the London and North Western, and in 1854 putting £20,000 in the Great Northern Railway, Darwin's income in the 1850s reached £5000 a year. Secure and self-financed, his days ran like clockwork, with set times for working, walking, lunching, napping, reading, letter writing, and nightly backgammon. His health remained precarious in the 1850s, and trips to London or social events brought on flatulence and vomiting.

Family duty for Darwin meant overriding his own dislike of the traditional public-school classical education and sending William (who until twelve was privately tutored in Latin by Henry Wharton, vicar of Mitcham, Surrey) to Rugby School in 1852. The family also had its duty: to support the patriarch, whose study became a sacred place. Nevertheless its boundary was often crossed by exuberant children asking for string or sticking plaster, or when a child was ill and settled on a sofa beside Darwin as he finished his work. The younger children had never known him do anything else and must have supposed that all

fathers were similarly employed, for one report-
edly enquired about a neighbour, 'Then where
does he do his barnacles?' (*More Letters*, 1.38).

Barnacles and natural selection

Darwin's first results appeared in 1851 in two
volumes on the stalked barnacles, *A Monograph
of the Fossil Lepadidae, or, Pedunculated Cirripedes of Great Britain*, published by the Palaeon-
tographical Society, and the 400-page *A monograph on the sub-class Cirripedia, with figures of
all the species: the Lepadidae, or, Pedunculated
cirripedes*, published by the Ray Society. The
latter reported Darwin's discovery of tiny 'com-
plemental males', as well as more contentious
points, particularly his view of the cement glands
as modified ovaria (which Thomas Henry Huxley
and, later, August Krohn were to disprove). For
his geological and barnacle volumes the Royal
Society awarded Darwin its Royal Medal in 1853,
and in 1854 he was elected to the Royal Society's
Philosophical Club and the Linnean Society. By
then he was finishing his work on the acorn-shell
barnacles, fascinated by abnormal types such as
the parasitic *Alcippe*, whose tiny males were little
more than reproductive organs in an envelope,

twelve of which could be found cemented to a female. These results were contained in the 684-page *A monograph on the sub-class Cirripedia, with figures of all the species: the Balanidae (or sessile cirripedes); the Verrucidae, etc.* (1854), and the shorter *A Monograph on the Fossil Balanidae and Verrucidae of Great Britain* (1854). In eight years Darwin had overhauled the entire subclass of fossil and living Cirripedia. He emerged not just an accredited geologist, but as a zoological specialist with authority to speak, when the time was ripe, on variability and transmutation.

This work brought Darwin into closer contact with Huxley, who had sent Darwin his early scientific papers and received from him a reference for a professorial chair. They probably first met in April 1853 at the Geological Society. Huxley, with Herbert Spencer, was part of a growing meritocratic, secularist network in London which was to make the world safe for Darwin's theories. These men, marginal to the Oxbridge–Anglican power structure, were recasting society and nature as a competitive market-place in the relaunched *Westminster Review*, seeking to claw power from a church establishment. The *Westminster* displayed the age's growing interest in laws of progress, division of labour, and questions of population and perfectibility, in society as in nature. Huxley, like Hooker, came round to transmutation after mid-decade, and Darwin recognized the importance of recruiting such men. However, although totally committed to natural selection, Darwin would still disarm correspondents by declaring that when he finally published, he would 'give all arguments & facts on both sides' (*Correspondence*, 5.294).

Late in 1854, after he finished the barnacle volumes, Darwin returned to collating his notes on species. He resolved one outstanding problem some time after November: how natural selection could force the branching of genera to give life's metaphorical 'tree'. Darwin explained this diverging of species as if it were the result of a division of labour; he proposed that natural selection favours those variants which diversify most from the original form. This was an industrial analogy, common in a decade of specializing workforces (personally familiar to Darwin from Wedgwood production-line practices) but also given meaning by the French zoologist Henri Milne-Edwards, whom Darwin cited. More directly, he came to this insight from statistical study of the relative proportions of species and genera in certain geographical areas, a study that led him to dwell on the problem of diversification and the maximum number of individuals that a plot of land could support. For Darwin, selection in nature's 'more efficient workshops' (Darwin, *Origin*, 1859, 380) would increase the 'physiological division of labour' over time. Competition for an overcrowded niche would favour variants that could exploit new opportunities. Dense populations would thus fan out on the spot, and in so doing mitigate the blending effects of back-breeding with the parent stock. Adding this 'principle of divergence' to his existing theories constituted a major intellectual shift for him, the most important alteration to his evolutionary scheme since writing the 1844 essay.

Darwin also tackled contemporary assumptions inimical to his theory. From 1855 he experimented to prove that seeds, plants, and animals could reach oceanic islands where they might produce new species in geographical isolation (in opposition to Joseph Dalton Hooker's belief in overland migration across former continental connections and land bridges, whose existence Darwin never accepted). To test the common notion that seeds were killed by seawater, he steeped kitchen garden seeds in brine and grew samples periodically to check their fertility. Then he attempted similar work with seeds specially chosen from lists of island plants supplied by Hooker and others. In the first of a series of notices in the *Gardeners' Chronicle*, Darwin announced that seeds germinated after forty-two days' immersion, which, given Atlantic currents, might see them floating 1400 miles, the distance to the Azores. He asked correspondents to watch for seeds or snails stuck to birds' feet; he floated dead pigeons bloated with seeds, raised seeds from bird droppings, and fed seed-stuffed sparrows to the snowy owl and Bateleur eagle at London Zoo in order to test the pellets for seed survival.

Like these dispersal experiments, Darwin's study of fancy pigeons from 1855 assumed a life of its own. Darwin joined the Philoperisteron and Borough pigeon clubs in London, corresponded with experts such as William Bernhard Tegetmeier and Bernard Brent, and built lofts at Down to house every fancy breed (in 1856 he had about ninety birds). His new contacts, and old friends such as his cousin Fox, gave him much practical help. Darwin himself became adept at dissecting nestlings and used natural selection to explain their embryonic similarity. The earlier in development the embryos were observed, the more they resembled the ancestral dove. He suggested that only dispositions to vary were inherited, the variations themselves appearing later when selection could operate. Embryos in the womb, untouched by selection, would thus look more alike than the divergent adults, such as pouters and runts. The way fanciers produced novel strains by accentuating chance variations through selective breeding (artificial selection) served as a powerful analogy for understanding Malthusian mechanisms in nature. Pigeons became part of Darwin's presentation strategy as well as evidence. Soon he was dissecting ducks and dogs. With Tegetmeier's advice he began a long-term programme of experimental crossing among different breeds of fowl, hoping to produce adults that reverted to the ancestral wild form. Darwin's use of animal husbandry, horticultural, and livestock manuals again set him apart from conventional specialists, whose descriptive, taxonomic enterprise disdained the farmyard.

The Origin of Species 5

For support Darwin was now looking primarily to the rising London men of science rather than Cambridge clerics. In April 1856 he invited T. H. Huxley to Down for a weekend party of naturalists, during which he hoped to ensure that his theory could overcome Huxley's objection to life's progressive specialization. After this meeting Darwin began writing for publication. He was encouraged by Charles Lyell, who feared for Darwin's priority after reading Alfred Russel Wallace's 'On the law which has regulated the introduction of new species' in the *Annals and Magazine of Natural History* for 1855. It was an opportune moment to publish, with the last radical scares—the Chartist marches and European revolutions of 1848—a fading memory, and with society liberalizing and the social basis of science shifting towards Huxley's professionals and secularists.

Darwin began writing on 14 May 1856, planning an extended technical treatise aimed at his peers. Within months his chapters were running to 100 pages. He suffered much anxiety and illness. He continued as Emma, aged forty-eight, gave birth to their last child, Charles Waring (1856–1858), who, according to Darwin's daughter Henrietta, lacked a 'full share of intelligence' and 'never learnt to walk or talk' (*Emma Darwin*, 2.162). During the period 1857–8 Darwin made four trips to Edward Lane's hydropathic establishment at Moor Park in Surrey, where he found a temporary respite from vomiting. He asked Hooker, Huxley, and John Lubbock to read parts of 'Natural selection', as he planned to call the book, and sent a summary dated 5 September 1857 to the Harvard University botanist Asa Gray. One aspect of his theory was now more pronounced: he no longer accepted organic beings as well adapted until conditions changed; rather, new variants were all to some degree imperfect and thus constantly struggling.

Still finding time to experiment and make natural history observations, Darwin studied the flight paths of humble-bees and tried to induce plant variations by rearing seeds under coloured glass or over-manuring the ground. He also solved, to his satisfaction, the problem of the evolution of the instincts of sterile worker bees. These left no offspring, so their instincts could not be selected. Darwin originally assumed that the sterile bees had been working queens that retained their instincts, but by 1857 he settled on another long-standing idea of his, 'family' selection, to explain the neuter castes. This assumed that the whole colony would benefit from any new adaptive instinct that appeared by chance among the sterile workers.

By March 1858 'Natural selection' was two-thirds complete, at 250,000 words, with the whole book projected to run to three volumes. It would carry the full weight of Darwin's scientific and social authority, which had increased in 1857 as the Academia Caesarea Leopoldino-Carolina Naturae Curiosum (the German academy of naturalists in Leipzig) elected him a member and the Kent commission of the peace swore him in as a justice of the peace. However, on 18 June he stopped abruptly, after receiving a letter from Wallace which enclosed an essay detailing Wallace's own seemingly identical theory. Wallace had corresponded with Darwin occasionally and sent him a few bird skins from the Malay archipelago. In previous letters they had touched on the species problem and Wallace enquired whether Darwin's book would tackle human origins (it would not, directly at least). Wallace had evidently singled Darwin out as potentially sympathetic to his own Malthusian explanation, devised in the spice islands in February 1858. More immediately, Wallace hoped that his essay would be passed on to Lyell, who had expressed interest in his earlier work. Although fearing loss of priority, Darwin did this and accepted Lyell's solution to the dilemma, which was to announce their theories jointly. Sick with worry—his infant son Charles Waring had developed scarlet fever and died on 28 June—Darwin left the arrangements to Lyell and Hooker. They presented extracts from Darwin's 1844 essay and excerpts from a copy of his 1857 letter to Gray, followed by Wallace's paper, at the Linnean Society on 1 July 1858. This double paper was published later that year as 'On the tendency of species to form varieties; and on the perpetuation of varieties and species by means of selection' in the *Journal of the Proceedings of the Linnean Society (Zoology)*. Events had moved so fast that

Wallace was not notified until afterwards. Darwin, greatly relieved by Wallace's courteous response, thereafter considered him one of the most generous of men: 'too modest, & how admirably free from envy or jealousy.—He must be a good fellow' (*Correspondence*, 8.218). This was the first public presentation of the theory of natural selection.

Darwin now moved quickly. On the Isle of Wight (where he had taken the ailing family), he started, at Hooker's urging, an 'abstract' of 'Natural selection' on 20 July 1858. First intended as an essay, it soon turned into a book. Recurrent stomach complaints and severe vomiting led to more bouts of water cure as Darwin passed his fiftieth birthday, but he pressed on to finish a manuscript of 155,000 words in April 1859. The book, stripped of references and academic paraphernalia, was aimed not at the specialists, but directly at the reading public. John Murray agreed to publish it sight unseen on Lyell's recommendation, although he did subsequently read the first three chapters and ask two respected friends to assess the completed manuscript. Darwin finished revising the proofs of *On the Origin of Species by Means of Natural Selection, or, The Preservation of Favoured Races in the Struggle for Life* 'as weak as a child'

(*Correspondence*, 7.328) and retreated to Ilkley Wells House spa, on the Yorkshire moors. He arranged with Murray to send out a large number of complimentary copies, and from his spa posted self-deprecating letters to many recipients of these copies, exclaiming typically, 'how you will long to crucify me alive' (*Correspondence*, 7.368). He described his time there, awaiting the outcome, covered in rashes and 'fiery Boils', as like 'living in Hell' (ibid., 7.362). He remained at the spa while Murray organized the trade sale of *Origin of Species* on 22 November 1859. The 1250 print-run was oversubscribed, requiring Murray to initiate a reprint. This permitted Darwin immediately to start collating corrections for a second edition. He was in Yorkshire on the presumed date of publication, Thursday 24 November (Freeman, *Works*, 75), returning home a fortnight later.

Darwin called the book 'one long argument', which he summarized thus:

If during the long course of ages and under varying conditions of life, organic beings vary at all in the several parts of their organization, and I think this cannot be disputed; if there be, owing to the high geometrical powers of increase of each species, at some age, season, or year, a severe struggle for life, and this certainly cannot be disputed; then, considering the infinite complexity of the relations of all organic beings to each other and to their conditions of existence, causing an infinite diversity in structure, constitution, and habits, to be advantageous to them, I think it would be a most extraordinary fact if no variation ever had occurred useful to each being's own welfare, in the same way as so many variations have occurred useful to man. But if variations useful to any organic being do occur, assuredly individuals thus characterised will have the best chance of being preserved in the struggle for life; and from the strong principle of inheritance they will tend to produce offspring similarly characterised. This principle of preservation, I have called, for the sake of brevity, Natural Selection... Amongst many animals, sexual selection will give its aid to ordinary selection, by assuring to the most vigorous and best adapted males the greatest number of offspring. Sexual selection will also give characters useful to the males alone, in their struggles with other males... Natural selection ... leads to divergence of character; for more living beings can be supported on the same area the more they diverge in structure, habits, and constitution, of which we see proof by looking at the inhabitants of any small spot or at naturalised productions. Therefore during the modification of the descendants of any one species, and during the incessant struggle of all species to increase in numbers, the more diversified these descendants become, the better will be their chance of succeeding in the battle of life. Thus the small differences distinguishing varieties of the same species, will steadily tend to increase till they come to equal the greater differences between species of the same genus, or even of distinct genera ... On these principles, I believe, the nature of the affinities of all organic beings may be explained. (Darwin, *Origin*, 1859, 127–8)

The rise of Darwinism

Reactions to *The Origin of Species*

The *Origin of Species* was applauded by Lyell, Hooker, Huxley, and others, and it impressed many younger men of science. Huxley's secular professionals and the literary radicals welcomed its thoroughgoing naturalism. For these reformers the *Origin* provided a dynamic biology to replace the old static, creationist hierarchy, while its progress through open competition defied Anglican–Oxbridge privilege. The chief Malthusian apologist, Harriet Martineau, talked of her 'unspeakable satisfaction' at the way Darwin had 'collected such a mass of facts, to transmute them by such sagacious treatment into such portentous knowledge' (*Harriet Martineau's Letters*, 186). But anti-Malthusians such as Karl Marx and Friedrich Engels were aghast at the way the *Origin* shadowed English political economy, however liberating its naturalism. On the other side, Adam Sedgwick was shocked that Darwin ignored providential design, although J. S. Henslow was more magnanimous. And the Christian socialist Charles Kingsley was content to follow Darwin's argument to some extent, believing that God had 'created primal forms capable of self-development into all forms needful pro tempore & pro loco' (*Correspondence*, 7.380). Others respected Darwin's evident sincerity and acknowledged his mass of factual material, while rejecting the argument wholesale.

In general Darwin's support within Anglicanism came from advanced liberals, often those who backed the broad-church manifesto *Essays and Reviews* (1860); indeed, they included one of the essayists, the Oxford geometry professor the Revd Baden Powell. Such support rested on the twin convictions that Darwin did not intend to subvert religious faith and that his work was based on genuine research. On the other hand, many critics drew the one conclusion that Darwin had avoided mentioning—that mankind was descended from apes—and castigated the book as dangerously irresponsible. Moreover the

'chance' appearance of variations and their utilitarian preservation, while horrifying detractors,
were difficult concepts even for many supporters,
including Huxley. One of those best qualified to
judge Darwin's work, the comparative anatomist
Richard Owen, delivered a crushing rebuttal
in the April 1860 *Edinburgh Review*, turning
Darwin's own words and facts against the *Origin*'s
conclusions. This review caused a permanent
breach in their relationship; Darwin felt personally offended as well as angry that his book had not
been given the serious assessment he thought it
deserved.

Darwin apparently still believed in a distant deity
and could speak of evolution being the result of
'designed laws' (*Correspondence*, 8.224), although
he did not mean the phrase providentially, but
rather in the Unitarian sense of a succession of
material causes running back to creation. But
he abstained from public controversy, preferring
that Huxley should tackle the *Origin*'s critics.
Huxley was confrontational; by alienating Owen
and the conservative clergy, he polarized the
debate. Darwin backed him none the less, even
while excusing himself from combat because of
illness. During Huxley's famous contretemps with

Bishop Samuel Wilberforce on 30 June 1860 at the Oxford meeting of the British Association for the Advancement of Science, Darwin was recuperating at Edward Lane's new water-cure establishment at Sudbrook Park in Surrey.

Darwin's theoretical work remained controversial among men of science. Thus, although he was nominated three years running for the Copley medal of the Royal Society, he was awarded it only in 1864. Even then it was amid furious politicking because, to Huxley's and Hooker's anger, the president, Edward Sabine, deliberately omitted the *Origin of Species* from the grounds of the award. But after 1866 'Darwinism' began to dominate the relevant sections of the British Association, where Darwin's chief scientific supporters, Hooker and Huxley, were presidents respectively in 1868 and 1870. However withdrawn, Darwin was adept at self-publicity, particularly to counteract hostile criticisms. He persuaded John Murray to publish a translation of Fritz Müller's *Für Darwin* (1864), subsidizing the project himself and targeting the review copies. This was a strategy that Darwin had already used successfully in arranging republication in Britain of Asa Gray's favourable reviews (*Natural Selection not Inconsistent with*

Natural Theology, 1861), and encouraging Henry Walter Bates to publish his evidence of natural selection among tropical butterflies. Darwin's attention also turned quickly towards overseas editions of the *Origin of Species*. The book was translated into French in 1862 by Clémence Royer (Darwin resented her alterations), and then by J. J. Moulinié in 1873 and Edouard Barbier in 1876; into German in 1860 by Heinrich Bronn (again disappointing Darwin) and 1862 by J. V. Carus; into Dutch in 1860 by T. C. Winkler, and then into Italian and Russian in 1864; Swedish in 1869; Danish in 1872; Hungarian and Polish in 1873–4; Spanish in 1877; and Serbian in 1878. After three pirate reprintings in New York before July 1860, Gray intervened and negotiated Appleton's official American editions with Darwin's blessing. The accounts for these transactions were carefully recorded by John Murray and Darwin.

Personal suffering

Darwin's health deteriorated again, beginning in September 1861. Lyell's failure to support evolution in his *Geological Evidences of the Antiquity of Man* (1863) provoked a further crisis, putting

Darwin 'in despair' (*More Letters*, 1.241) and sending him back to Dr Gully at Malvern. Darwin's vomiting was now accompanied by severe headaches, which increased his isolation. At times he was too weak even to walk in the garden or write, and he dictated to Emma. From April 1865 he suffered eight months of appalling illness and was bedridden for some of the time. His symptoms remained primarily gastro-intestinal, including extensive nausea, indigestion, skin inflammations, flatulence, and vomiting, often accompanied by headaches, tiredness, irregular sleeping patterns, occasional giddy spells, and faintness. He became a recluse for several years and developed the fixed habits of an invalid. Doctors came and went, sometimes overlapping. One was the rationalist John Chapman, editor of the *Westminster Review* and a specialist in psychological problems among the intelligentsia, who treated Darwin with ice-bags on the spine; this was to no avail and Darwin again looked elsewhere. His physicians ranged from eminent metropolitan doctors to water-cure practitioners. Most of them suggested special diets or medications to make Darwin's stomach fluids more alkaline. Henry Bence Jones diagnosed 'suppressed gout' and advised brisk exercise. Darwin complied for a year or two by horse-riding, but this ceased in 1869 after his horse fell on Keston Common, throwing Darwin.

A ruddy complexion and sturdy physique often masked Darwin's suffering. In middle life he was about 6 feet tall, with a slight stoop. His son Francis records that he had an average build and long thin legs, which he crossed completely when seated (*Life and Letters*, ed. Darwin, 1.108–60). His eyes were blue-grey and he wore pince-nez spectacles in later years for reading and experimenting. Though hirsute, he became quite bald, with only a fringe of dark untidy hair behind. After 1862 he grew a full beard, partly to soothe recurrent facial eczema, and this so altered his appearance that friends failed to recognize him when he briefly appeared in society in 1866. His voice was a thin tenor, rather like his father's, and his laugh a hearty peal. When excited he became thoroughly animated, gesturing frequently, especially when explaining a complex point, and he tended to speak in fragmentary sentences. He often complained about the difficulties he experienced in writing connected scientific prose and gratefully received help from family members and friends. From boyhood he had a habit of moving his fingers rapidly in parallel and, if very excited, raising both hands to the sides of his face, fingers still fidgeting. To control this, when seated, he would hold one wrist with the other hand, but even in later life the habit would take over as he paced the Sandwalk.

In October 1866 Darwin met his chief German supporter, Ernst Haeckel of Jena University. For Haeckel the trip to Down House was like a religious pilgrimage. Gray and his wife, visiting in 1868, commented on the house's frayed and workaday interior and Darwin's rhythmical daily routine, ending in the obligatory evening game of backgammon, but not even their host's 'merriest laugh' could disguise the ravages of 'suffering and disease' (J. L. Gray to S. L. Jackson, 28 Oct 1868, Gray Herbarium, Harvard University). The same year, while holidaying on the Isle of Wight, Darwin was introduced to Alfred Tennyson, the American poet Henry Wadsworth Longfellow, and the photographer Julia Margaret Cameron, for whom Darwin sat for a fine set of portraits. With the *Origin of Species* in half a dozen foreign translations, Darwin had the order of merit conferred on him by the king of Prussia and was elected a corresponding member of the Imperial Academy of Sciences at St Petersburg. In 1870 Oxford University offered him an honorary doctorate of civil laws, but this was rejected by Darwin on grounds of ill health, and the Imperial Society of Naturalists in Moscow made him an honorary member. The Church of England's South American Missionary Society did the same, recognizing that Darwin, keen to see civilization spread in Tierra del Fuego, had made small donations for several years.

In later editions of the *Origin of Species* Darwin somewhat tempered the power of natural selection. The physicist William Thomson (Lord Kelvin) calculated the age of the earth as 100 million years or less since crustal condensation, while Darwin mooted 300 million years since Cretaceous times. With natural selection relying on the rare appearance of minute advantageous variations, the new shorter term required an acceleration of the evolutionary process. In the fifth edition of the *Origin* (1869), Darwin allowed that a number of useful variations might have been induced by changing environments and that 'use-inheritance', or the inheritance of beneficial characteristics acquired during an individual's life, played a larger part in adaptive change. These *ad hoc* devices also helped to meet the engineer Fleeming Jenkin's objection about the swamping effects of blending inheritance, but, for bringing them into play in the *Variation* as well as the *Origin*'s later editions, Darwin was accused of resorting to Lamarckian causes, even though, in reality, he had never entirely foresworn them. The words 'I am convinced that Natural Selection has been the main [or 'most important'] but not exclusive means of modification' conclude the introductory chapter in each edition of the *Origin of Species* (1859, 1860, 1861, 1866, 1869, 1872). For all the changes in detail, overall its main thesis stood firm.

Variation of Animals and Plants

After the *Origin*'s publication Darwin embarked on two broad lines of research: botanical experiments, and studies of variation, sexual selection, and emotional expressions in humans and mammals. In 1860 he began recycling the early, as yet unpublished, chapters of 'Natural selection' and studying the osteology of domestic pigeons, ducks, and geese for a book on how breeders and horticulturists modify species. This was *The tion* (1868), which progressed only slowly. Its two volumes were intended to provide overwhelming evidence for the ubiquity of variation, although they would also incidentally answer Lyell and Gray, who maintained that variations had not occurred purely by chance but were providentially directed. Darwin showed that breeders indeed selected from a vast array of minute random variations. He gave numerous instances of the causes of variability, including the direct effect of the conditions of life, reversion, the effects of use and disuse, saltation, prepotency, and correlated growth.

The *Variation* also addressed a key criticism of the *Origin of Species*: that it lacked an adequate understanding of inheritance. Darwin's 'provisional hypothesis of pangenesis' was constructed to explain how heritable truths were passed from parents to offspring. He supposed that each part of a parent organism throws off minute particles, or 'gemmules', which circulate in the body and collect in the sexual organs to be transmitted in reproduction. Because gemmules are received from two parents, the offspring develop to resemble them both more or less. 'The child, strictly speaking, does not grow into the man, but includes germs which slowly and successively become developed and form the man' (Darwin, *Variation*, 1875 edn, 2.398). Darwin's hypothesis was roundly criticized, most tellingly by his cousin Francis Galton, who transfused pure-colour rabbits with the blood of other varieties to show that gemmules were not present in the blood. However, Darwin denied that his hypothesis required blood to bear the gemmules. On a different question Jenkin argued in 1867 that natural selection was powerless to preserve individual favourable variants if characteristics were always blended in inheritance. Any variants appearing in a freely interbreeding population would soon be swamped and disappear. This argument gave Darwin considerable trouble, his pangenesis hypothesis notwithstanding. It was only later, with Moritz Wagner's insistence on geographical isolation in the evolutionary process (a notion itself developed from Darwin's work), that the blending problem looked as if it was solved.

The term 'survival of the fittest' (borrowed at Wallace's insistence from Herbert Spencer's 1866 *Principles of Biology*) first appeared in the *Variation* and in the fifth edition of the *Origin of Species*

(1869). It was a partial substitute for Darwin's more anthropomorphic 'natural selection', which many critics took to imply the existence of a 'selector'. Mistaking Darwin's metaphor, they concluded that intelligence lay as much behind nature's selecting as behind a pigeon fancier's. Nevertheless Darwin defended his use of 'natural selection' while conceding that he had personified it too much.

The *Variation* was a full statement of the facts on which the theories of the *Origin* were based. Darwin, 'taunted that I concealed my views' (*Life and Letters*, ed. Darwin, 3.98) on human origins, had at first intended to include a chapter on mankind, fleshing out his old notebook conviction that humans had evolved like other animals. But before *Variation* was published he gave up this plan and decided to treat the topic separately. Still reluctant to speak out, he had hoped that either Lyell, Huxley, Lubbock, or Wallace would publish a full-blooded account of human evolution, but none came up to expectation. Accordingly, in February 1868, he started sorting his huge collection of notes and began a two-volume treatise, *The Descent of Man, and Selection in Relation to Sex* (1871).

While writing Darwin differed sharply from Wallace over mental development and sexual selection. Wallace, a convert to spiritualism, in 1869 explained the savage's expansive brain as a spiritually guided preadaptation for civilization, thus limiting natural selection to the earlier physical origin of human races. Darwin, dismayed, wrote to him, 'I hope you have not murdered too completely your own and my child' (Marchant, 1.241). Similarly, Wallace denied the existence of sexual selection, the adjunct cause that Darwin had introduced to account for characteristics with no physically adaptive functions, such as human beards or humming-bird iridescence. Wallace's critique went to the heart of the arguments in the *Descent of Man*, for Darwin believed that sexual selection also accounted for the differentiation of human races.

Other critics had to be answered. The Catholic comparative anatomist St George Mivart published articles in *The Month* in 1869 denying that natural selection could explain the independent 'convergence' of animal forms (such as a placental dog and Australian thylacine) or that the intermediate stages of certain structures (such as a wing) could be functional and thus formed by selection. Moreover, the duke of Argyll in *Primeval Man* (1869) argued that mankind had more likely fallen from some higher state than risen from animals. He questioned how selection could have produced a weak-framed, hairless human, at least without morality and reason having been bestowed first. But Darwin turned the logic around: it was this physical vulnerability, he said, that had forced humans into social groups whose cohesion and altruism were themselves responsible for the continuing evolution of morality.

By 1871, when the *Descent of Man* was published, Darwinism had become a byword among intellectuals and the preceding decade had seen the public habituated to writings on ape ancestry by Huxley, Wallace, Karl Vogt, and Haeckel, and on the evolution of civilization by Galton, Lubbock, Edward Tylor, W. R. Greg, and Walter Bagehot. Much of their work—which reinforced conventional racial, national, and sexual prejudices— was incorporated into the *Descent of Man*. Darwin also extended his notebook themes of the natural origin of morality, religious belief, and society from animal instincts and savage superstitions.

The *Descent*, understood by Darwin as a sequel to the *Origin*, was written with a maturity and depth of learning that marked Darwin's status as an élite gentleman of science. Despite its title, less than half of the book dealt with mankind. Some two-thirds was devoted to a description of sexual selection in the animal kingdom, leading Wallace to complain that it was really two books. Yet sexual selection was an answer to those critics who saw peacock tails as an expression of divine aesthetics—beauty as an end in itself and incapable of natural explanation. Darwin also set out a definite family tree for humans, tracing their affinity with the Old World monkeys. He provided a survey of aboriginal societies to establish that each held its own ideal of beauty. For he believed that, during prehistory, such distinct ideals of beauty, when preserved with other useful traits by long-continued sexual selection, had led to the divergence of the human races. Darwin laid out his views on the evolutionary origins of morality and religion, and illustrated those aspects in which 'Man still bears in his bodily frame the indelible stamp of his lowly origin'. Indeed, he

> The early progenitors of man were no doubt
> once covered with hair, both sexes having
> beards; their ears were pointed and capable of
> movement; and their bodies were provided with
> a tail, having the proper muscles ... The foot,
> judging from the condition of the great toe in
> the foetus, was then prehensile; and our progen-
> itors, no doubt, were arboreal in their habits
> (Darwin, *Descent*, 1.206)

While perhaps causing less of an outcry than
the *Origin*, the *Descent of Man* brought the full
force of evolutionary proposals directly into the
heart of ordinary Victorian life. It sold more than
5000 copies within a year and provoked numerous
press caricatures, cartoons, articles, and commen-
taries. A second edition appeared in 1874 and
eight translations were published during Darwin's
lifetime.

Darwin was sensitive to Mivart's renewed criticism in *On the Genesis of Species* (1871) and determined to break off communication with him. (He
did so in 1874 after Mivart accused Darwin's son
George of advocating the loosening of marriage

bonds in cases where there was a threat to the 'fitness' of offspring.) In 1871 Darwin arranged for an article by the American philosopher Chauncey Wright rebuking Mivart to be reprinted as a pamphlet under the title *Darwinism*. At this time the *Origin* was also extensively rewritten to answer Mivart. The sixth and last edition explained how, for instance, swim bladders were preadapted to function as lungs, obviating the need to talk of half-formed organs. In this edition the word 'evolution', used in its modern sense, first appeared.

One batch of material proved too bulky for incorporation in the *Descent of Man* and Darwin held it over for separate treatment. This derived from his research into human and animal expressions. The subject had fascinated him since his London days, and had drawn him many times to the zoological gardens to watch the monkeys and apes. Later he had recorded his children's behaviour, investigated facial expressions of the insane, consulted artists and photographers, and collected material on the exterior manifestation of emotional states such as happiness or rage. The material was sophisticated for its day. Darwin invited the photographer Oscar Rejlander to make comparative studies of laughter and crying; he obtained photographs of lunatics from asylum director James Crichton-Browne; and he consulted the French physiologist Guillaume Duchenne about his electrical research on facial muscles. Believing that learned expressions could be 'fixed' by habit, Darwin also formulated his clearest statement to date on the inheritance of acquired characteristics. Though much of his analysis has been superseded, and was for modern scientific purposes marred by much unconscious anthropomorphism, he was convinced that an evolutionary continuity existed between the expressions (and hence mental life) of animals and humans, and that animals experience traces of every human emotion, including the moral feelings. In this sense, *The Expression of the Emotions in Man and Animals* (1872) completed his great cycle of evolutionary writings. It proved popular, not least because of its accessible subject matter and plentiful illustrations, including some of the earliest commercially reproduced photographs in a printed book.

Botany and belief, 1861–1882

Botanical observations

During the controversy over the *Origin of Species* Darwin increasingly turned to botanical observations. He had always considered plants as important to his theories as animals: many of the arguments for adaptation, variation, and descent in the *Origin* hinged on his early botanical work, particularly in plant geography. He was a regular contributor to *Gardeners' Chronicle* and sent papers on botanical topics to the Linnean Society of London. After publishing the *Origin* he carried out a wide range of investigations into the living processes of plants and their adaptations. He usually characterized these researches as a pleasant rest or amusement, apparently feeling that they interrupted the hard work of compiling his big book on variation. He often remarked that he was not a 'proper' botanist, by which he meant a taxonomic expert like his friends Joseph Dalton Hooker and Asa Gray, but his pleasure in experimenting with plants was obvious. The stream of books and papers that he published during the last twenty years of his life was greatly admired by botanists, earning him a reputation as a gifted observer and ingenious botanical thinker. When Darwin was elected a corresponding member of the Académie des Sciences in Paris in 1878, it was specifically to the botanical section. From 1873 he was helped by his son Francis who wrote several works with him. (Francis continued various projects after his father's death, and produced amended editions of some of Darwin's books.) Despite Darwin's humorous protestations, every aspect of his botanical work, however trivial it appeared, bore closely on adaptation, variation, and the origin of species by natural selection.

Many of Darwin's research projects began with observations made in his garden or while on holiday. In 1860 he experimented on the sundew, an insectivorous plant that he noticed while resting in Sussex. He continued the work intermittently until 1875 when he published *Insectivorous Plants*, which discussed the whole range of such plants, their adaptations and evolutionary relationships, and their specialized digestive processes. On holiday at Torquay in 1861 he took up the fertilization of orchids, a subject that had long intrigued him; this resulted in *On the Various Contrivances by which British and Foreign Orchids are Fertilised by Insects* (1862). Darwin called the book a 'flank movement' (*Correspondence*, 10.331) on the enemy, meaning that it tackled the question of design in nature. He maintained that the ornate ridges and horns of orchid flowers, and the complex internal arrangements, were not beauty for its own sake, or created for the delight of humans, but adaptations to facilitate reproduction. They existed to ensure cross-pollination by insects. If they were regarded as functional flowers, rather than beautiful ones, natural selection could explain their origin. Among Darwin's striking discoveries was his revelation that three well-known species of the orchid *Catasetum* were actually a single species existing in three forms, male, female, and hermaphrodite. He distinguished such relationships by comparing the gradual separation of the sexes with a similar process he had described in barnacles.

Examples of mutual adaptation between insects and flowers tantalized Darwin and he continued to research into orchids and many other plant–insect relationships, especially those involving bees. He had first read C. K. Sprengel's *Das entdeckte Geheimniss der Natur im Bau und in der Befruchtung der Blumen* (1793) on the advice of Robert Brown in 1841 and he thought it 'a wonderful book' (*Autobiography*, 127). His own work involved many small experiments in his garden, masking and unmasking flowering plants during the summer season. In the winter of 1862–3 his orchid research led him to build the first of several hothouses in which he could keep delicate research specimens obtained from Hooker at Kew and other specialists in Britain and abroad.

From the early 1840s he had suspected that cross-pollinated plants tended to leave more vigorous offspring than those which were self-fertilized. One long-term aim was to show how far plants had adapted to ensure this crossing. After the *Origin* he performed experiments on dozens of species and hundreds of plants, sometimes to the tenth generation, to establish that crossing conferred selective advantage, which he usually measured by counting or weighing seeds. In this work he relied on the experimental plant-hybridizing results of K. F. von Gärtner, J. G. Koelreuter, and latterly K. W. Nägeli. In *The Effects of Cross and Self-Fertilisation in the Vegetable Kingdom* (1876) he showed statistically that the offspring of crosses are more vigorous than seedlings of self-fertilized parentage and thus more likely to survive. The advantage in developing mechanisms that prevented selfing or in transforming hermaphroditic systems into bisexual structures was quantified for the first time. Darwin's further work on the evolution of two sexes expressed a similar interest. He investigated the two forms of primula, long styled and short styled, which he concluded in 1862 were more fertile when crossed. In 1865 he published on *Lythrum salicaria*, the purple loosestrife, which has three forms of flower: having experimented to induce 'illegitimate unions' (*Collected Papers*, 2.120) among them, he assessed the increased sterility of the offspring and showed how the flowers functioned to effect cross-pollination. These and other experiments were reported in papers at the Linnean Society and then in *The Different Forms of Flowers on Plants of the Same Species* (1877), which was dedicated to Gray in gratitude for decades of encouraging correspondence.

There was perhaps more to Darwin's lifelong fascination with in- and out-breeding than met the eye. Married himself to a first cousin, and both of them from a line with its share of perceived physical or mental anomalies, he feared that he carried a weakness, most evident in his chronic ill health. After his daughter Anne's death in 1851, and long years of sickness among his remaining children, he became convinced that his 'detestable constitution' (*Correspondence*, 7.60) had been passed to the next generation. So urgent was the subject to him, with its social-evolutionary implications, that he tried—unsuccessfully—to get a question on first-cousin marriages and their offspring placed on the 1871 national census return through the good offices of his friend Sir John Lubbock, who had become MP for Maidstone the previous year.

Darwin was also intrigued by the more energetic aspects of plant physiology. While ill in 1863 he studied the circular movements of pea tendrils as they searched for an object to twine around. He went on to examine over 100 species of climbers, publishing the results in 1865 as a Linnean Society monograph and in 1875 under the same title, *The Movements and Habits of Climbing Plants*.

In the wild, he surmised, the climbing adaptation aided survival in dense vegetation. Assisted by his son Francis he widened the research to survey the movements of stems, leaves, and roots under the influence of gravity, moisture, and light. Darwin believed that in plants an inherent tendency to move had been intensified and diversified by natural selection. His interpretation of geotropism (the response of roots to gravity) in *The Power of Movement in Plants* (1880) contradicted the results of Julius Sachs, stimulating an argument that disintegrated into a nationalistic contest between Darwin's old-style country-house observations and the new laboratory-based physiological research emerging in the German states. Despite Sachs's criticism, Darwin never wavered in his belief that a substance in the tip of a shoot was activated by light, a belief that gave impetus to subsequent studies on plant hormones. His experimental equipment in all these investigations was makeshift. Darwin took pride in the *ad hoc* nature of his practical researches, frequently praising his simple apparatus over the fine gadgetry available to younger university workers. All the same, he purchased several expensive microscopes, justifying the expense as 'essential'.

Although Darwin's achievement in botany was long underestimated, his chief aim was to show the power of evolutionary theory for understanding plant morphology and physiology. Many people who might have shied away from ape-ancestry were prepared to accept natural selection and evolution among plants. His botanical books, however, were not as widely read or appreciated as the others.

Religion and politics

Solidly wealthy, in the 1870s Darwin was reinvesting over half of his annual income of £8000. His affection for his closest friends remained intense: he felt Lyell's death in 1875 keenly, and played a leading part in arranging a collection of funds in 1873 to permit an exhausted Huxley to take a rest from his duties. He enthusiastically supported the foundation of the zoological station at Naples, under Anton Dohrn, and donated £100 for equipment in 1879. In his will he provided £250 annually for the completion of a catalogue of all known plants, the *Index Kewensis*. Darwin continued his parish duties until the early 1870s, donating funds to the church and vicarage, but after 1871 a new vicar at Downe (as it was

increasingly being spelled) turned the school com-
mittee and parish education towards the Thirty-
Nine Articles, causing Darwin to withdraw his
support.

In 1881 the impecunious Alfred Russel Wallace
received a civil list pension of £200 at Darwin's
instigation and with the Liberal government's
approval. Nevertheless, the two old men never
fully appreciated one another's political and
cultural views; while remaining friends, they
moved apart intellectually. Darwin deplored Wallace's spiritualism. With séances all the rage he
and Emma Darwin did attend one in 1874 at
his brother Erasmus's house, along with Galton,
Henrietta and Richard Litchfield (Darwin's son-
in-law), Hensleigh and Fanny Wedgwood, and
George Lewes and Marian Evans (George Eliot).
Darwin's son George hired the medium, Charles
Williams. Darwin retired upstairs before the per-
formance, denouncing it all as 'rubbish' (*Life and
Letters*, ed. Darwin, 3.187).

Though a rationalist, Darwin was cautious of
mooting his religious views lest he offend or be
offended in turn. He did give an endorsement
to the freethinking platform of Francis Abbot's

American newspaper *The Index* in 1871, only to regret his public support when atheism became an issue in Britain with Charles Bradlaugh's case in 1880. He had the endorsement removed. While admitting 'I do not believe in the Bible as a divine revelation, & therefore not in Jesus Christ as the Son of God' (Darwin to F. McDermott, 24 Nov 1880, Cambridge University Library), Darwin also confessed that he had 'never been an atheist in the sense of denying the existence of a God', and 'that generally (& more & more as I grow older), but not always, that an agnostic would be the most correct description of my state of mind' (*Life and Letters*, ed. Darwin, 1.304). Thus Edward Aveling's request in 1880 to dedicate a book to Darwin was turned down on the grounds that:

> though I am a strong advocate for free thought on all subjects, yet it appears to me (whether rightly or wrongly) that direct arguments against christianity & theism produce hardly any effect on the public; & freedom of thought is best promoted by the gradual illumination of men's minds, which follow[s] from the advance of science. (Feuer, 2–3)

Darwin disapproved of socialists, ultra-radicals, and neo-Malthusians (that is, birth-controllers)

no less than atheists, spiritualists, and bishops.
When Bradlaugh and Annie Besant asked if
they might subpoena him in 1877 to appear at
their trial for publishing contraceptive advice,
Darwin threatened to denounce their views.
A Malthusian struggle was the cornerstone of
natural selection, and he opposed those who
diminished it by 'any means' (Darwin, *Descent*,
2.403). 'The rule insisted on by all our Trades-
Unions, that all workmen,—the good and bad,
the strong and weak,—sh[ould] all work for the
same number of hours and receive the same
wages' rather than be paid by 'piece-work' was,
he insisted, 'opposed ... to all competition. I fear
that Cooperative Societies... likewise exclude
competition. This seems to me a great evil for the
future progress of mankind' (Weikart, 611). Yet he
also said that looking after the weak and sick was
a defining characteristic of 'civilized' societies.

For all his antipathy to extremes, Darwin in
his autobiography, 'Recollections of the development of my mind and character', written for
the family in stages through 1876, 1879, and
1881, frankly stated his conviction that the doctrine of eternal damnation for unbelief was
itself 'damnable'. (This passage, and others, were

omitted for Emma's sake when the autobiography was first published in *The Life and Letters of Charles Darwin*.) In 1876 Francis Darwin moved back into Down House with his infant son Bernard after the death of his wife, so that Darwin's last years were spent with a grandchild, in whom he took great delight. In 1879 Darwin also wrote an introduction to Ernst Krause's biography of his grandfather Erasmus Darwin on its translation into English, which elicited a sharp attack from the author and artist, Samuel Butler.

The Liberal press, led by John Morley, long supported Darwin, and he remained a staunch Gladstonian Liberal himself. From 1865 he supported Lubbock (later first Baron Avebury) when he stood at Maidstone as Liberal MP, and he took intense political and humanitarian interest in the American Civil War, discussing it vigorously in letters to Gray. In 1876 Darwin signed up as one of the convenors of the St James's Hall demonstration against the massacre of 15,000 Bulgarian rebels by Turkish troops (the 'Bulgarian horrors'), and agreed with Gladstone that the Russians should secure Christian Bulgaria against the Turks. Darwin also supported professional science, backing the comparative anatomists and medical men in their fight for vivisection. He helped draft a bill enabling vivisection under licensed conditions, which he sent to Lord Derby. At Huxley's request, he appeared as a witness in 1875 before the royal commission on the practice of subjecting live animals to experiments.

Final years

During these autumn years Darwin's health improved and his honours multiplied. In 1877 Cambridge University bestowed an honorary doctorate of laws on him. When he did not go into the world, it came to him: Gladstone visited Down House in 1877, accompanied by the Liberal lights Lyon Playfair, Morley, Lubbock, and Huxley. No archive sources have been found to show that Darwin was suggested for a knighthood (despite an unsubstantiated rumour that his name had been put forward before the publication of the *Origin of Species*). Many thought it shameful that the British establishment signally failed to honour him. Only in 1881 did Gladstone belatedly offer him a trusteeship of the British Museum. It was a rare, and minor, show of state recognition, and one of the very few official duties ever offered to him, but Darwin turned it down. He sat for the artist

John Collier (1881), the oil portrait being commissioned by the Linnean Society. By special invitation he dined with the prince of Wales and leading physicians at the seventh International Medical Congress in 1881. By then he had returned to a subject that he had mulled over since the 1830s, the action of earthworms in causing great earth movements. It was his leitmotif, explaining vast changes by minute incremental events: mountain uplift, evolving life, and now worms transforming the soil. More ingenious experiments—including testing worms' sensitivity to sound, light, and shape—culminated in *The Formation of Vegetable Mould through the Action of Worms* (1881).

In June 1881 an attempt at a mountain walk on holiday in the Lake District left Darwin feeling faint, and angina was diagnosed. Enforced idleness made him miserable; insatiably curious, he needed some new intellectual peak, but he had climbed them all. At Christmas that year he had a minor heart attack on the steps of his protégé George Romanes's house in Regent's Park, London. Another seizure followed on 7 March 1882 as he hobbled round the Sandwalk, with a further series on 4 and 5 April. He died, in great suffering, at Down House on 19 April 1882, aged seventy-three. On his brother Erasmus's death the previous year (and burial in Downe church-yard), Darwin had inherited half of his estate and became personally worth over a quarter of a million pounds. His new will bequeathed £34,000 to each of his daughters, £53,000 to each son, and £1000 each to Hooker and Huxley. His oldest son, William, a banker, was the executor.

Following agitation by Galton and Huxley among the cultural and scientific élite, and with a petition raised by Lubbock in the House of Commons, plans were made to bury Darwin in Westminster Abbey, although he himself had expected to lie in Downe churchyard. A press campaign compared Darwin to Isaac Newton and evoked imperial and patriotic feelings, and Darwin's intellectual conquests were seen to equal the great Victorian geographical annexations: 'we owe it to posterity to place his remains in Westminster Abbey, among the illustrious dead who make that noble fane unrivalled in the world' (*The Standard*, 22 April 1882). On 26 April 1882 Darwin was buried in the abbey, close to the monument to Newton at the north end of the choir screen, in a ceremony attended by the elders of science, state, and church.

Darwin's legacy

8

Claiming and debating Darwin

Agnostic scientists, Liberal politicians, and broad-churchmen joined in paying homage to one who, though an unbeliever, symbolized Britain's success in conquering nature and civilizing the globe during Victoria's reign. They consolidated Darwin's most enduring image. In their speeches, sermons, and memoirs, the Kentish squire and patriarch became the iconic scientist—detached, objective, a lone seeker after truth, released by personal wealth and stoic dedication in the face of long-continued illness to bestow priceless truths on humanity. By the end of the century everyone wanted this Darwin as an ally. From secularists to salvationists, from Prussian nationalists to Russian anarchists, efforts continued to enlist his authority by appealing to his life and works.

Darwin's personal reputation did not guarantee the success of his ideas. The *Origin of Species*, never out of print, was translated into at least thirty-six languages, but its theories were often too materialistic for idealists and too capitalistic for socialists, too empiricist for Germans and too English for the French. Not even his key belief, the one he himself most emphasized, 'change of species by descent' (*Correspondence*, 11.402–3), was accepted *in toto*. Many of his avowed disciples, including scientists, exempted 'man' from evolution by supposing that the human mind or soul was added to an animal body. More ironically, for over half a century the distinctive core of Darwin's science, his arguments for natural and sexual selection, came under sustained fire. Natural selection, if anything, was construed as a negative force rather than creative, a purging of unfit organisms shaped by Lamarckian use–inheritance, macromutation, or evolution's inner directing energy. Sexual selection was explained away or found inapplicable to human beings. Even among Darwin's closest allies, Huxley never allowed that natural selection had been proved, but evolution *per se* became an academic commonplace, and in 1909 leading scientists gathered on both sides of the Atlantic to mark

Darwin's centenary with speeches and public
celebrations.

So 'Darwinism', a term first publicized by Huxley, and increasingly used during Darwin's lifetime, was contested from the start. Efforts to restrict its meaning to natural selection pure and simple or 'what Darwin taught' proved futile as later critics and commentators exploited the textual changes in the *Origin*'s six editions. Soon after Darwin's death publications brought his private letters to the fore. Everywhere Darwinism became synonymous with naturalism, materialism, or evolutionary philosophy. It stood for competition and co-operation, liberation and subordination, progress and pessimism, war and peace. Its politics could be liberal, socialist, or conservative, its religion atheistic or orthodox. At the turn of the twentieth century European social scientists, then American, began using 'social Darwinism' as a shorthand for biological theories that impinged on their professional domain. The phrase all but disappeared at the end of the First World War but in the 1940s American liberals revived it as a label for *laissez-faire* ideology as found in the works of Darwin's contemporary, the English philosopher Herbert Spencer, and his latter-day followers.

Social Darwinism then became a sin from which Darwin himself had to be absolved. Great pains were taken during the cold war to show that the sources of his science, no less than his own motives and beliefs in writing the *Origin*, were ideologically pure.

The issue was made more urgent by what the early twentieth century saw perpetrated in Darwin's name. While in Britain his cousin Galton's campaign for national eugenics had only marginal political impact, events took a sinister turn on the continent: from Ernst Haeckel to Adolf Hitler, German imperialist readings of the *Origin*'s subtitle, 'the preservation of favoured races in the struggle for life', sanctioned unthinkable suffering and played into anti-Darwinian hands. In communist Russia from the late 1930s, no less than in fundamentalist America after the First World War, Darwin's theories were vilified for their degrading effects. (Only much later was the full extent of eugenic practices, East and West, revealed.) Thus besieged liberals in the mid-twentieth century maintained that Darwin had been persistently misread, his theories misapplied, his science 'misused' by partisans on all sides, and that, properly

understood, Darwin had taught nothing politically untoward.

Many defenders of a non-ideological Darwin also saw themselves as his true successors. This placed them in awkward company. From the time of Darwin's death, natural selection had been upheld chiefly by biometricians such as W. F. Weldon and Karl Pearson, whose experimental and statistical researches buttressed Galton's eugenics. Darwin's sons George, Leonard, and Horace also supported Galton and the eugenics movement; Leonard specially encouraged the young R. A. Fisher, who in 1918 showed that Darwinian selection could harness Mendelian genetics to solve eugenic problems. It was Fisher's *The Genetical Theory of Natural Selection* (1930) and the collateral work of J. B. S. Haldane in England and Sewall Wright in the United States that made possible the 'evolutionary synthesis' of the 1930s. With further contributions by Theodosius Dobzhansky, Julian Huxley, Ernst Mayr, G. G. Simpson, and G. Ledyard Stebbins, natural selection was then reformulated in terms of mathematical population genetics, and a generation of evolutionists in the 1950s happily positioned themselves 'closer ... to the Darwin of 1859 than at any other period in the last 100 years' (Mayr, 'Introduction', viii). In centenary celebrations for the *Origins of Species*, they hailed the book's first edition for precipitating a 'Darwinian revolution' in which natural selection had in principle defeated all competing evolutionary mechanisms. Darwin the iconic scientist, whose theories had long been attacked and politically abused, was revalued as the founder of an ascendant 'neo-Darwinism' and the patron saint of modern biology.

Yet this apparent vindication of a non-ideological Darwin was inextricably bound up with moral and metaphysical issues, as indeed Darwin's own work had been from the start. In the 1970s and 1980s, with the hardening of the neo-Darwinian synthesis in the new fields of sociobiology and evolutionary psychology, the pattern persisted. Despite the efforts of Stephen Jay Gould, the most popular and historically minded of Darwinian scientists in the late twentieth century, biologists' attachment to Darwin's theories assumed a quasi-theological character. Natural selection to them became a deity *manqué*, a 'blind watchmaker' that fills 'design space' with marvellous adaptations. After the collapse of Soviet communism ended the cold war in the 1990s, some sympathizers and many pundits urged political progressives to seek fresh inspiration for the new millennium, not from Karl Marx, but from Darwin.

Darwin's life in print

A large and increasingly technical literature has grown up around Darwin's life and works. From the outset, interpreters were indebted to his family for preserving and publishing key manuscripts—Darwin's memory was well served by his children. The seven who reached adulthood survived to see his 1909 centenary celebrations in London and Cambridge, in which the sons were honoured guests. Francis Darwin edited an exceptional three-volume *Life and Letters* (1887), two further volumes of his father's correspondence with the assistance of A. C. Seward (1903), and the two unpublished early drafts of the theory of natural selection (1909). Francis also published a one-volume *Life* (1892) and Henrietta Litchfield, the eldest daughter, prepared two volumes of her mother's family letters, which were printed privately in 1904 and published in 1915.

While the children lived their memories and opinions shaped Darwin's public image. They adored him, and interpreters deferred to their authority. The Darwins were conspicuous among the intermarried extended families that dominated British intellectual life and politics at the end of the nineteenth century. They held sway in Cambridge, where George Darwin became Plumian professor of astronomy, Francis a reader in botany, and Horace a founder and director of the Cambridge Scientific Instrument Company and later mayor. All married well and had families. In 1964 the George Darwin family residence, Newnham Grange, became the home of Darwin College, the first Cambridge college for postgraduates. Of Darwin's nine grandchildren, all but one survived past mid-century. Nora Barlow, the youngest child of Horace Darwin, published five important transcripts of Darwin's manuscripts, including his *Beagle* diary (1933) and ornithological notes (1963), and the full autobiography (1958), of which only the expurgated *Life and Letters* version had been known. A great-grandson descended through George Darwin, Richard Darwin Keynes, re-edited the *Beagle* diary (1988) and published the zoological notes and specimen lists from the *Beagle* voyage (2000). From the 1920s family members were also active in helping to preserve the Down House estate as a national shrine. The

house was rented by Down House School (1907–
22), then (through the bequest of Sir George Buckston-Browne) passed to the British Association in 1929. In 1953 it was given to the Royal College of Surgeons of England, from whence it was transferred to the Natural History Museum, and from 1996 it was restored and run as a public museum by English Heritage.

For the first half of the twentieth century scholars studied Darwin primarily as a thinker who had 'forerunners' or 'precursors' and whose ideas were either 'revolutionary' or 'in the air'. His life was treated as an episode in intellectual history. Scientists made him a reference point in debates about evolutionary theory, humanists portrayed him as a great (though perhaps dangerous) moralist, and religious commentators as a theological saint or satan. In the 1940s the Darwin family began depositing a wealth of manuscripts and other biographical material, including Darwin's working library, at Cambridge University Library, but for years this went almost untapped as interpreters dwelt on Darwin's published work and its place in the history of ideas. At its best, this concentration yielded authoritative studies such as Ellegård's *Darwin and the General Reader* (1958), about the reception of Darwin's ideas in the British periodical press. One of the most widely read and evocative studies of Darwin from this period was William Irvine's *Apes, Angels, and Victorians* (1955).

Reassessments of Darwin's life accompanied the neo-Darwinian re-evaluation of natural selection celebrated on the centenary of the *Origin of Species* in 1959. Much of the enthusiasm surrounding this centenary and its publications rested on the assumption that a theory recognized as true must have a history different from one written when its status was in doubt. Scientists dealt severely with a professional historian, Gertrude Himmelfarb, whose important *Darwin and the Darwinian Revolution* (1959) failed sufficiently to recognize the new status of natural selection. But much interest was also focused on Darwin because, to mark the centenary, Gavin De Beer, the retired director of the British Museum (Natural History), began publishing Darwin manuscripts, including the private notebooks that recorded his earliest thoughts about transmutation. This was a watershed. A generation of historians of science, professionalizing themselves since the Second World War, then began to exploit the Darwin papers at Cambridge. The 'Darwin industry' was born.

Darwin in history and context

De Beer's concise biography (1963) was the last major attempt by a working scientist to interpret Darwin's life as history. Although efforts continued to enlist Darwin's authority in debates about evolution—the most tenacious and influential scientist–commentator into the twenty-first century was Ernst Mayr, an architect of the evolutionary synthesis—within two decades the field was crowded with historical specialists. A strong shift in approach was signalled by the vigorous work of R. M. Young, published from 1967 onwards. Philosophers and philosophically minded historians such as Ghiselin, Hull, R. J. Richards, and Ruse analysed Darwin's logic, methodology, and metaphysics, but most crucially historical specialists led by Kohn, Hodge, Gruber, Barrett, Herbert, Manier, and Schweber offered particularly fruitful readings of Darwin's early manuscripts. Darwin's debts to Robert Edmond Grant and the 'Grantian' social and scientific context were elucidated by Sloan and Desmond, while Sloan demonstrated how Darwin's first evolutionary theorizing in 1837 took shape in response to Richard Owen's work. Sulloway carefully reconstructed Darwin's ornithological collections from the Galápagos and thereby re-evaluated the timing of Darwin's appreciation of island speciation. Limoges wrote carefully about natural selection and Ospovat's *The Development of Darwin's Theory* (1981) studied its relations with mid-nineteenth-century biology. Vorzimmer traced the theory's vicissitudes through the six editions of the *Origin of Species* into the *Descent of Man*.

Much of the historians' interest lay in the discovery of natural selection, but their research held little for the champions of Darwin's methodological rectitude. The notebooks revealed the young Darwin reaching out in all directions, to physics, philosophy, political economy, and theology, as well as to collectors, breeders, museum keepers, and field naturalists. 'Conjecture run wild' (Barrett and others, *Notebooks*, B232) or 'mental rioting' (*Correspondence*, 4.40), he called it. By the 1980s historians had shown that natural selection was no classic 'discovery', but rather a slow, painstaking 'construction' (La Vergata, 917) from diverse cultural resources. Their work—in

particular the detailed reconstructions of Darwin's
zig-zagging path to natural selection by Kohn and
Hodge—marked an epoch in Darwin research.
No longer could it be claimed that Darwin was
the iconic scientist conforming to methodological
ideals past or present. His originality lay in his
idiosyncrasy.

Central to Darwin's theorizing was his effort
to explain the descent of human beings—body,
mind, and society—from ape-like animals on the
basis of a materialist or monist metaphysics and
using Malthus's 'principle of population'. This was
clear from De Beer's edition of the transmutation
notebooks, and from early work by Herbert, and in
1974 Gruber and Barrett published further manuscripts, including two notebooks ('M' and 'N') in
which he speculated about 'metaphysics', 'morals',
and 'expression'. Here at last was compelling evidence that 'man' lay at the core of his work from
the start. Darwin did not first formulate natural selection and then apply it to human beings;
he drew the theory directly from contemporary
(and ideologically loaded) assessments of human
behaviour and afterwards concealed its implications for over three decades, until the *Descent of
Man.*

Much historical ink was spilt in the mid-twentieth century (surveyed by Oldroyd in 1984) over the question of Darwin's debt to Malthus. Thanks to the notebooks, particularly the monumental new edition published in 1987 by Barrett, Gautrey, Herbert, Kohn, and Sydney Smith, and to commentators such as Gruber, Schweber, and Ospovat, interpretations once dismissed as externalist or even Marxist were found more congenial. Few now could doubt that (as Greene first demonstrated) Darwin was as much a social evolutionist as Spencer, with whom he had often been contrasted. Moreover, the emergence in the late 1970s and 1980s of sophisticated social studies of science, fortified by Desmond's re-evaluation of the medical and scientific context of Darwin's key creative period in the 1830s, permitted greater flexibility in understanding the meaning of Malthusian science in Darwin's day, his potential audience, and his reluctance to publish his theory. As Darwinian studies proliferated, historians turned to re-examine other figures in the history of evolutionary theory, notably Chambers, Huxley, Spencer, and Lamarck. Their analyses in turn cast important new light on Darwin's Victorian context.

Moore reassessed Darwin's religious faith, showing that while he remained a pillar of his rural parish, the deaths of his father in 1848 and daughter Annie in 1851 finally led him to give up Christianity. Brown offered a different view, while Ospovat, Kohn, and Gillespie traced the vicissitudes of Darwin's theology. Beddall and Kottler re-examined Darwin's relations with Alfred Russel Wallace, analysing differences and the question of illicit borrowing. Browne, Kohn, and Ospovat reinterpreted his 'principle of divergence' and Secord recast Darwin's breeding work as social history. Browne analysed his biogeography and Ekman assessed his research on expression. Barrett, Herbert, Rudwick, and Secord offered new interpretations of Darwin's geology. Darwin's non-evolutionary and non-geological research also came in for detailed study, including his insect collecting by K. G. V. Smith, his barnacle taxonomy by Sydney Smith, Ghiselin, and Newman, and his plants by Porter. Legends were laid to rest: Gruber and Burstyn disposed of Darwin as the *Beagle*'s official naturalist (he was the captain's gentleman companion); Sulloway demoted Darwin's Galápagos finch-collecting from its previous evolutionary eureka-point status; P. Thomas Carroll, Colp, Feuer, and others showed that it was not Marx's offer of the dedication in volume two of *Das Kapital* that Darwin refused in a famous letter; and Moore exposed the fundamentalist story that Darwin gave up evolution and professed Christianity on his deathbed. Detailed studies of Darwin's reception in France, Italy, Germany, Russia, Spain, China, North America, and the Arab world were also published, including comparative works edited by Glick, and Numbers and Stenhouse.

So from the 1970s, revisionist views proliferated on every aspect of Darwin's life and work. His long post-*Beagle* illness was much debated but its nature never fully resolved. Early complaints such as eczema and heart palpitations possibly foreshadowed a permanent disorder, and some later symptoms certainly suggest the possibility of an underlying physical defect such as an ulcerated gut, allergies, or a neurological or metabolic malfunction. In any case, both before and during the *Beagle* voyage Darwin displayed hearty good health. Only after 1837, when he moved to London and began theorizing about transmutation, does his correspondence chart an

increasingly persistent series of nausea-related
conditions. These lifted during his last decade,
after the *Descent of Man* appeared, and he died
of heart failure brought on by old age.

Interpretations of the illness broadly support
either physical or psychosomatic causation and
thus themselves chart controversies in medical
knowledge. Pickering's influential suggestion in
1974, that Darwin's condition should be regarded
as a 'creative malady' that allowed him time to
get on with his work, was a view partly expressed
by Darwin himself and mooted by his younger
contemporaries. As an invalid needing peace and
privacy, he chose to conduct much of his scientific work through correspondence. He withdrew
from the administrative side of science at an early
age and constantly found excuses to avoid society.
During the mid-1860s, when he was severely ill,
colleagues visited Down House only infrequently
and Emma forbade them to linger. Yet Darwin's
symptoms were real enough and he regularly
complained that sickness was keeping him from
his work. Over the years he offered so many
excuses that even his own words must be inter-
preted with caution.

Medical authorities joined the debate, particularly after the 1959 centenary. The parasitologist Saul Adler's suggestion that Darwin contracted Chagas's disease while in Chile was repeatedly discounted on archival grounds. In a full review of the literature, Colp, a psychiatrist, proposed in 1977 that Darwin suffered from stress-related conditions induced by his private study of transmutation and his fears about the public controversy it would provoke. At one point Darwin himself declared, 'my abstract [the *Origin of Species*] is the cause, I believe of the main part of the ills to which my flesh is heir' (*Correspondence*, 7.247). This psychosomatic aetiology has been widely accepted, and in 1998 Colp acknowledged Chagas's disease as a likely predisposing cause. Bowlby, a child psychiatrist, considered the death of Darwin's mother when he was eight years old highly significant for his future health. Many other interpretations have been offered, all more or less likely. The subject's endless interest may be partly explained by the traditional association of creative genius with intense mental agitation. Darwin's personal equanimity and calm private life, however, stand in sharp contrast to the social and intellectual turmoil provoked by his work.

Darwin for today

When scientists and historians marked the centenary of Darwin's death in 1982 their views of Darwin were as disparate as their commemorative publications. Kohn's 1000-page collection, *The Darwinian Heritage* (1985), surpassed all others as the most tangible evidence to date that responsibility for shaping Darwin's image had passed to historians. The study of his life and works was now a specialism as rigorous and exacting as any in the life sciences, and indeed by 1990 scholars possessed an array of sophisticated tools for constructing an entirely fresh portrait of Darwin: the newly edited *Beagle* diary (1988) and transmutation notebooks (1987); the 'big book' ('Natural selection') from which the *Origin of Species* was condensed (1975); a variorum *Origin* edited by Peckham (1959); Darwin's collected papers (1977); his marginalia transcribed by Di Gregorio and Gill (1990); concordances to the *Origin* (1981), *Descent of Man* (1987), and *Expression of the Emotions* (1986) supervised by Barrett; a bibliographical handlist (1977; supplement 1986) and biographical 'companion' (1978) compiled by Freeman; and a calendar of some 15,000 letters to and from Darwin (1985; revised edn 1994) together with *The Correspondence of*

Charles Darwin (1985–), edited by a transatlantic team under the guidance of Burkhardt and, until his death, Sydney Smith. The thirty-two projected volumes of the *Correspondence*, due for completion about 2025, will keep biographers busy well into the twenty-first century.

In 1990 new biographies based on these rich resources began to appear. Though they differ (often sharply) from one another, and none should be called definitive, they mark the abandonment of intellectual hagiography. Scholars now concern themselves less with Darwin as a heroic thinker than as a Victorian gentleman–naturalist who had the time, income, and nerve to touch the untouchable and make evolution culturally acceptable. This turn towards histories that offer more deeply informed, socially embedded explanations of Darwin's career and influence is clear evidence that the study of Western science, its history and social relations, reached new levels of professionalism by the start of the twenty-first century.

Sources

Biographies

J. Browne, *Charles Darwin*, 2 vols (1995–2002) · A. Desmond and J. Moore, *Darwin* (1991) · P. J. Bowler, *Charles Darwin: the man and his influence* (1990) [with historiographic survey] · J. Bowlby, *Charles Darwin: a biography* (1990) · G. Himmelfarb, *Darwin and the Darwinian revolution* (1959) · P. Brent, *Charles Darwin: a 'man of enlarged curiosity'* (1981) · G. De Beer, *Charles Darwin: evolution by natural selection* (1963) · W. Irvine, *Apes, angels, and Victorians: the story of Darwin, Huxley, and evolution* (1955)

Texts and tools

Charles Darwin's notebooks, 1836–1844: geology, transmutation of species, metaphysical enquiries, ed. P. H. Barrett and others (1987) [transcription of Darwin's notebooks; with index and bibliography] · *The correspondence of Charles Darwin*, ed. F. Burkhardt and S. Smith, [15 vols.] (1985–) · *The collected papers of Charles Darwin*, ed. P. H. Barrett, 2 vols. (1977) [Darwin's periodical articles, omitting only a few; with index and bibliography] · *The autobiography of Charles Darwin, 1809–1882*, ed. N. Barlow (1958) · *Charles Darwin's Beagle diary*, ed. R. D. Keynes (1988) [annotated transcription] · C. Darwin, *The works of Charles Darwin*, ed. P. H. Barrett and R. B. Freeman, 29 vols. (1986–9) [with bibliography] · F. Burkhardt and S. Smith, eds., *A calendar of the correspondence of Charles Darwin, 1821–1882* (1985); rev. edn (1994) · T. Junker and M. Richmond, eds., *Charles Darwins Briefwechsel mit deutschen*

Naturforschern: ein Kalendarium mit Inhaltsangaben, biograph-
ischen Register und Bibliographie (1996) · *The life and letters of*
Charles Darwin, ed. F. Darwin, 3rd edn, 3 vols. (1887) · *More*
letters of Charles Darwin, ed. F. Darwin and A. C. Seward, 2 vols.
(1903) · *Emma Darwin: a century of family letters, 1792–1896*, ed.
H. Litchfield, 2 vols. (1915) [privately printed, 1904] · H. E. Gruber
and P. H. Barrett, *Darwin on man: a psychological study of scientific*
creativity ... together with Darwin's early and unpublished note-
books (1974) · S. Herbert, ed., *The red notebook of Charles Darwin*
(1980) · *Charles Darwin's 'Natural selection': being the second part*
of his big species book written from 1856 to 1858, ed. R. C. Stauffer
(1975) · M. A. Di Gregorio and N. W. Gill, *Charles Darwin's mar-*
ginalia, 1 (1990) [transcription of annotations in Darwin's scientific
library] · *Charles Darwin's diary of the voyage of H.M.S. 'Beagle'*,
ed. N. Barlow (1933) · *Charles Darwin's zoology notes and specimen*
lists from H.M.S. 'Beagle', ed. R. D. Keynes (2000) · N. Barlow,
ed., 'Darwin's ornithological notes', *Bulletin of the British Museum*
(Natural History), Historical Series, 2 (1963), 201–78 · C. Darwin,
On the origin of species by means of natural selection, or, The preser-
vation of favoured races in the struggle for life (1859) · C. Darwin,
The descent of man, and selection in relation to sex, 2 vols. (1871) ·
C. Darwin, *The variation of animals and plants under domestication*,
2 vols. (1868); rev. edn (1875) · *The foundations of 'The origin of*
species': two essays written in 1842 and 1844, ed. F. Darwin (1909) ·
R. B. Freeman, *The works of Charles Darwin: an annotated bibli-*
ographical handlist, 2nd edn (1977); suppl. (1986) [standard bibli-
ography] · R. B. Freeman, *Charles Darwin: a companion* (1978) ·
R. B. Freeman, *Darwin pedigrees* (1984) · M. Peckham, ed., *The*
'Origin of species' by Charles Darwin: a variorum text (1959) · P. H.
Barrett, D. J. Weinshank, and T. Gottleber, eds., *A concordance*
to Darwin's 'Origin of species', first edition (1981) · P. H. Barrett,
D. J. Weinshank, P. Ruhlen, and S. J. Ozminski, eds., *A concordance*
to Darwin's 'The descent of man, and selection, in relation to sex'
(1987) · P. H. Barrett, D. J. Weinshank, P. Ruhlen, S. J. Ozminski,
and B. M. Berghage, eds., *A concordance to Darwin's 'The expression*
of emotions in man and animals' (1986) · L. Huxley, *Life and letters*
of Joseph Dalton Hooker, 2 vols. (1918) · L. Huxley, *Life and letters*
of Thomas Henry Huxley, 2 vols. (1900) · J. Marchant, *Alfred*
Russel Wallace: letters and reminiscences, 2 vols. (1916) · R. Keynes,

(2001) · E. Healey, *Emma Darwin: the inspirational wife of a genius* (2001) · R. B. Freeman, 'The Darwin family', *Biological Journal of the Linnean Society*, 17 (1982), 9–21 · parish register, Shrewsbury, St Chad's, 17 Nov 1809 [baptism] · parish register, Maer, St Peter's, 29 Jan 1839 [marriage] · death certificate

Interpretative studies

D. Kohn, ed., *The Darwinian heritage* (1985) · D. Kohn, 'Theories to work by: rejected theories, reproduction, and Darwin's path to natural selection', *Studies in History of Biology*, 4 (1980), 67–170 · F. J. Sulloway, 'Darwin and his finches: the evolution of a legend', *Journal of the History of Biology*, 15 (1982), 1–53 · F. J. Sulloway, 'Darwin's conversion: the *Beagle* voyage and its aftermath', *Journal of the History of Biology*, 15 (1982), 325–96 · P. R. Sloan, 'Darwin's invertebrate program, 1826–1836: preconditions for transformism', *The Darwinian heritage*, ed. D. Kohn (1985), 71–120 · P. R. Sloan, 'Darwin, vital matter, and the transformism of species', *Journal of the History of Biology*, 19 (1986), 367–95 · D. Ospovat, *The development of Darwin's theory: natural history, natural theology, and natural selection, 1838–1859* (1981) · M. J. S. Hodge, 'Darwin and the laws of the animate part of the terrestrial system (1835–1837): on the Lyellian origins of his zoonomical explanatory program', *Studies in History of Biology*, 7 (1983), 1–106 · A. Desmond, *The politics of evolution: morphology, medicine and reform in radical London* (1989) · J. Moore, 'Darwin of Down: the evolutionist as squarson-naturalist', *The Darwinian heritage*, ed. D. Kohn (1985), 435–81 · R. Colp, *To be an invalid: the illness of Charles Darwin* (1977) · J. Secord, 'Darwin and the breeders: a social history', *The Darwinian heritage*, ed. D. Kohn (1985), 519–42 · D. Kohn, 'Darwin's ambiguity: the secularization of biological meaning', *British Journal for the History of Science*, 22 (1989), 215–39 · E. Richards, 'Darwin and the descent of woman', *The wider domain of evolutionary thought*, ed. D. R. Oldroyd and I. Langham (1983), 57–111 · J. C. Greene, 'Darwin as a social evolutionist', *Journal of the History of Biology*, 10 (1977), 1–27 · B. G. Beddall, 'Darwin and divergence: the Wallace connection', *Journal of the History of Biology*, 21 (1988), 1–68 · J. R. Moore, 'Of love and death: why Darwin "gave up Christianity" ', *History, humanity and*

evolution, ed. J. R. Moore (1989), 195–229 · D. Kohn, 'The aesthetic
construction of Darwin's theory', *The elusive synthesis: aesthetics
and science*, ed. A. I. Tauber (1996), 13–48 · M. J. S. Hodge and
D. Kohn, 'The immediate origins of natural selection', *The Darwinian heritage*, ed. D. Kohn (1985), 185–206 · M. J. S. Hodge,
'Darwin as a lifelong generation theorist', *The Darwinian heritage*, ed. D. Kohn (1985), 207–43 · M. J. S. Hodge, 'The structure
and strategy of Darwin's "Long Argument" ', *British Journal for
the History of Science*, 10 (1977), 237–46 · R. Colp, ' "To be an
invalid", redux', *Journal of the History of Biology*, 31 (1998), 211–
40 · R. Colp, ' "Confessing a murder": Darwin's first revelations
about transmutation', *Isis*, 77 (1986), 9–32 · R. Keynes, *Fossils,
finches and Fuegians: Charles Darwin's adventures and discoveries
on the* Beagle, *1832-1836* (2002) · J. A. Secord, 'Nature's fancy:
Charles Darwin and the breeding of pigeons', *Isis*, 72 (1981), 163–
86 · J. Browne, 'Darwin's botanical arithmetic and the principle
of divergence, 1854–1858', *Journal of the History of Biology*, 13
(1980), 53–89 · D. Kohn, 'Darwin's principle of divergence as
internal dialogue', *The Darwinian heritage*, ed. D. Kohn (1985),
245–57 · J. Moore, 'Freethought, secularism, agnosticism: the case
of Charles Darwin', *Traditions* (1988), vol. 1 of *Religion in Victorian
Britain*, ed. G. Parsons, 274–319 · E. Manier, *The young Darwin and
his cultural circle: a study of the influences which helped shape the
language and logic of the first drafts of the theory of natural selection*
(1977) · C. Limoges, *La sélection naturelle: étude sur la première
constitution d'un concept (1837–1859)* (1970) · S. Herbert, 'The place
of man in the development of Darwin's theory of transmutation,
part 1, to July 1837', *Journal of the History of Biology*, 7 (1974), 217–
58 · S. Herbert, 'The place of man in the development of Darwin's
theory of transmutation, part 2', *Journal of the History of Biology*,
10 (1977), 155–227 · G. Jones, 'The social history of Darwin's
"Descent of man" ', *Economy and Society*, 7 (1978), 1–23 · M.
Kottler, 'Charles Darwin and Alfred Russel Wallace: two decades of
debate over natural selection', *The Darwinian heritage*, ed. D. Kohn
(1985), 367–432 · S. S. Schweber, 'Darwin and the political econo-
mists: divergence of character', *Journal of the History of Biology*,
13 (1980), 195–289 · S. S. Schweber, 'The origin of the "Origin"
revisited', *Journal of the History of Biology*, 10 (1977), 229–316 ·
H. L. Burstyn, 'If Darwin wasn't the *Beagle*'s naturalist, why was he

on board?', *British Journal for the History of Science*, 8 (1975), 62–9 · J. W. Gruber, 'Who was the *Beagle*'s naturalist', *British Journal for the History of Science*, 4 (1968–9), 266–82 · N. Hazelwood, *Savage: the life and times of Jemmy Button* (2000) · F. W. Nicholas and J. M. Nicholas, *Charles Darwin in Australia, with illustrations and additional commentary from other members of the Beagle's company, including Conrad Martens, Augustus Earle, Captain FitzRoy, Philip Gidley King, and Syms Covington* (1989) · P. Armstrong, *Charles Darwin in Western Australia: a young scientist's perception of an environment* (1985) · P. Armstrong, *Darwin's desolate islands: a naturalist in the Falklands, 1833 and 1834* (1992) · P. Armstrong, *Under the blue vault of heaven: a study of Charles Darwin's sojourn in the Cocos (Keeling) Islands* (1991) · P. Armstrong, *Charles Darwin's last island: Terceira, Azores, 1836* (1992) · J. A. Secord, 'The discovery of a vocation: Darwin's early geology', *British Journal for the History of Science*, 24 (1991), 133–57 · M. Rudwick, 'Charles Darwin in London: the integration of public and private science', *Isis*, 73 (1982), 186–206 · S. Herbert, *Charles Darwin, geologist* (2005) · S. Herbert, 'Darwin the young geologist', *The Darwinian heritage*, ed. D. Kohn (1985), 483–510 · J. Browne, 'Darwin and the expression of the emotions', *The Darwinian heritage*, ed. D. Kohn (1985), 307–26 · J. Browne, 'I could have retched all night: Charles Darwin and his body', *Science incarnate: historical embodiments of natural knowledge*, ed. C. Lawrence and S. Shapin (1998), 240–87 · J. Moore, 'Charles Darwin lies in Westminster Abbey', *Biological Journal of the Linnean Society*, 17 (1982), 97–113 · L. S. Feuer, 'Is the "Darwin–Marx correspondence" authentic?', *Annals of Science*, 32 (1975), 1–12 · R. Colp, 'The myth of the Darwin–Marx letter', *History of Political Economy*, 14 (1982), 461–82 · R. Weikart, 'A recently discovered Darwin letter on social Darwinism', *Isis*, 86 (1995), 609–11 · M. J. S. Rudwick, 'Darwin and Glen Roy: a "great failure" in scientific method?', *Studies in the History and Philosophy of Science*, 5 (1974), 97–185 · P. H. Barrett, 'The Sedgwick–Darwin geologic tour of north Wales', *Proceedings of the American Philosophical Society*, 118 (1974), 146–64 · J. Browne, *The secular ark: studies in the history of biogeography* (1983) · J. Browne, 'The Charles Darwin–Joseph Hooker correspondence: an analysis of manuscript resources and their use in biography', *Journal of the Society of the Bibliography of Natural History*, 8 (1976–8),

351–66 · A. C. Love, 'Darwin and cirripedia prior to 1846: exploring the origins of the barnacle research', *Journal of the History of Biology*, 35 (2002), 251-89 · W. A. Newman, 'Darwin and cirripedology', *Crustacean Issues*, 7 (1993), 349–434 · K. G. V. Smith, ed., 'Darwin's insects: Charles Darwin's entomological notes', *Bulletin of the British Museum (Natural History)*, Historical Series, 14 (1987), 1–143 · D. M. Porter, ed., 'Darwin's notes on *Beagle* plants', *Bulletin of the British Museum (Natural History)*, Historical Series, 14 (1987), 145–233 · D. R. Stoddart, 'Darwin, Lyell, and the geological significance of coral reefs', *British Journal for the History of Science*, 9 (1976), 119–218 · P. Ekman, ed., *Darwin and facial expression: a century of research in review* (1973) · S. de Chadarevian, 'Laboratory science versus country-house experiments: the controversy between Julius Sachs and Charles Darwin', *British Journal for the History of Science*, 29 (1996), 17–41 · F. B. Brown, *The evolution of Darwin's religious views* (1986) · D. Amigoni and J. Wallace, eds., *Charles Darwin's 'The origin of species': new interdisciplinary essays* (1995) · P. J. Vorzimmer, *Charles Darwin, the years of controversy: the 'Origin of species' and its critics, 1859–82* (1970) · E. Mayr, 'Introduction', in C. Darwin, *On the origin of species by natural selection: a facsimile of the first edition, with an introduction by Ernst Mayr* (1964) · S. Smith, 'The origin of the "Origin" as discerned from Charles Darwin's notebooks and his annotations in the books he read between 1837 and 1842', *Advancement of Science*, 16 (1960), 391–401 · H. Atkins, *Down, the home of the Darwins: the story of a house and the people who lived there*, rev. edn (1976) · J. H. Ashworth, 'Charles Darwin as a student in Edinburgh, 1825–1827', *Proceedings of the Royal Society of Edinburgh*, 55 (1934–5), 97–113 · G. Shepperson, 'The intellectual background of Charles Darwin's student years at Edinburgh', *Darwinism and the study of society*, ed. M. Banton (1961), 17–35 · S. M. Walters and E. A. Stow, *Darwin's mentor: John Stevens Henslow, 1796-1861* (2001) · J. J. Parodiz, *Darwin in the New World* (1981) · W. F. Cannon, 'The impact of uniformitarianism: two letters from John Herschel to Charles Lyell, 1836–1837', *Proceedings of the American Philosophical Society*, 105 (1961), 301–14 · N. C. Gillespie, *Charles Darwin and the problem of creation* (1979) · M. Ruse, *The Darwinian paradigm: essays on its history, philosophy, and religious implications* (1989) · E. Mayr, *One long argument: Charles Darwin and*

Darwinian method (1969) · S. Adler, 'Darwin's illness', *Nature*, 184
(1959), 1102–3 · G. Pickering, *Creative malady: illness in the lives*
and minds of Charles Darwin, Florence Nightingale, Mary Baker
Eddy, Sigmund Freud, Marcel Proust, Elizabeth Barrett Browning
(1974) · *Harriet Martineau's letters to Fanny Wedgwood*, ed. E.
Sanders Arbuckle (1983)

Darwin's influence

A. Ellegård, *Darwin and the general reader: the reception of*
Darwin's theory of evolution in the British periodical press, 1859–
1872 (1958) · R. M. Young, *Darwin's metaphor: nature's place in*
Victorian culture (1985) · G. Beer, *Darwin's plots: evolutionary*
narrative in Darwin, George Eliot, and nineteenth-century fiction
(1983) · J. Gayon, *Darwinism's struggle for survival: heredity and*
the hypothesis of natural selection (1998) · P. J. Bowler, *The eclipse of*
Darwinism: anti-Darwinian evolution theories in the decades around
1900 (1983) · T. Glick, ed., *The comparative reception of Darwinism*
(1974) · R. L. Numbers and J. Stenhouse, eds., *Disseminating Dar-*
winism: the role of place, race, religion, and gender (1999) · D. C.
Bellomy, ' "Social Darwinism" revisited', *Perspectives in Amer-*
ican History, new ser., 1 (1984), 1–129 · S. Shapin and B. Barnes,
'Darwin and social Darwinism: purity and history', *Natural order:*
historical studies of scientific culture, ed. S. Shapin and B. Barnes
(1979), 125–42 · P. Crook, *Darwinism, war and history: the debate*
over the biology of war from the 'Origin of species' to the First
World War (1994) · M. Hawkins, *Social Darwinism in European*
and American thought, 1860–1945: nature as model and nature as
threat (1997) · P. Tort, ed., *Darwinisme et société* (1992) · R. J.
Richards, *Darwin and the emergence of evolutionary theories of*
mind and behavior (1987) · D. Oldroyd and I. Langham, eds., *The*
wider domain of evolutionary thought (1983) · J. R. Moore, *The*
post-Darwinian controversies (1979) · J. Moore, 'Deconstructing
Darwinism: the politics of evolution in the 1860s', *Journal of the*
History of Biology, 24 (1991), 353–408 · J. Roberts, *Darwinism and*
the divine in America: protestant intellectuals and organic evolution,
1859–1900 (1988) · R. L. Numbers, *Darwinism comes to America*
(1998) · P. Corsi and P. J. Weindling, 'Darwinism in Germany,

France, and Italy', *The Darwinian heritage*, ed. D. Kohn (1985), 683–729 · T. Junker, *Darwinismus und Botanik: Rezeption, Kritik und theoretische Alternativen im Deutschland des 19. Jahrhunderts* (Stuttgart, 1989) · J. Hodge and G. Radick, eds., *The Cambridge companion to Charles Darwin* (2003) · Y. Conry, *L'introduction du darwinisme en France au XIXᵉ siècle* (1974) · G. Pancaldi, *Darwin in Italy: science across cultural frontiers* (1991) · A. Kelly, *The descent of Darwin: the popularization of Darwinism in Germany, 1860–1914* (1981) · D. P. Todes, *Darwin without Malthus: the struggle for existence in Russian evolutionary thought* (1989) · A. Vucinich, *Darwin in Russian thought* (1988) · R. MacLeod and P. Rehbock, eds., *Darwin's laboratory: evolutionary theory and natural history in the Pacific* (1994) · T. Glick, *Darwin en España* (1982) · A. A. Ziadat, *Western science in the Arab world: the impact of Darwinism, 1860–1930* (1986) · J. R. Pusey, *China and Charles Darwin* (1983) · P. J. Bowler, *Evolution: the history of an idea* (1984) · P. J. Bowler, *The non-Darwinian revolution: reinterpreting a historical myth* (1988) · D. L. Hull, *Darwin and his critics: the reception of Darwin's theory by the scientific community* (1973) · E. Mayr and W. B. Provine, *The evolutionary synthesis: perspectives on the unification of biology* (1980) · V. B. Smocovitis, *Unifying biology: the evolutionary synthesis and evolutionary biology* (1996) · V. B. Smocovitis, 'Celebrating Darwin: the Darwin centennial celebration at the University of Chicago', *Osiris*, 2nd ser., 14 (1999), 1–66 · J. Moore, *The Darwin legend* (1994) · D. S. Bendall, ed., *Evolution from molecules to men* [Cambridge 1982] (1983) · Y. Conry, ed., *De Darwin au darwinisme: science et idéologie* [Paris, Chantilly 1982] (1983) · S. Tax and C. Callender, eds., *Evolution after Darwin: the University of Chicago centennial*, 3 vols. (1960) · A. C. Seward, ed., *Darwin and modern science: essays in commemoration of the centenary of the birth of Charles Darwin and of the fiftieth anniversary of the publication of 'The origin of species'* (1909) · American Association for the Advancement of Science, *Fifty years of Darwinism: modern aspects of evolution: centennial addresses in honour of Charles Darwin before the American Association for the Advancement of Science, Baltimore, Friday, January 1, 1909* (1909) · W. G. Ridewood, ed., *Memorials of Charles Darwin: a collection of manuscripts, portraits, medals, books and natural history specimens to commemorate the centenary of his birth and*

Literature surveys

A. La Vergata, 'Images of Darwin: a historiographic overview', *The Darwinian heritage*, ed. D. Kohn (1985), 901–72 · I. Bohlin, 'Through Malthusian specs? A study in the philosophy of science studies with special reference to the theory and ideology of Darwin historiography', PhD diss., University of Göteborg, 1995 · D. Oldroyd, 'How did Darwin arrive at his theory? The secondary literature to 1982', *History of Science*, 22 (1984), 325–74 · J. Moore, 'Socializing Darwinism: historiography and the fortunes of a phase', *Science as politics*, ed. L. Levidow (1986), 38–80 · J. Moore, 'On revolutionizing the Darwin industry: a centennial retrospect', *Radical Philosophy*, no. 37 (1984), 13–22 · I. Bohlin, 'R. M. Young and Darwin historiography', *Social Studies of Science*, 21 (1991), 597–648 · R. Colp, 'Charles Darwin's past and future biographies', *History of Science*, 27 (1989), 167–97 · F. B. Churchill, 'Darwin and the historian', *Biological Journal of the Linnean Society*, 17 (1982), 45–68 · T. Lenoir, 'The Darwin industry', *Journal of the History of Biology*, 20 (1987), 115–30 · J. C. Greene, 'Reflections on the progress of Darwin studies', *Journal of the History of Biology*, 8 (1975), 243–73 · M. Ruse, 'The Darwin industry: a critical evaluation', *History of Science*, 12 (1974), 43–58 · D. C. Bellomy, ' "Social Darwinism" revisited', *Perspectives in American History*, new ser., 1 (1984), 1–129

Index

Enjoy biography? Explore more than 55,000 life stories in the Oxford Dictionary of National Biography

The biographies in the 'Very Interesting People' series derive from the *Oxford Dictionary of National Biography*—available in 60 print volumes and online.

To find out about the lives of more than 55,000 people who shaped all aspects of Britain's past worldwide, visit the *Oxford DNB* website at **www.oxforddnb.com**.

There's lots to discover ...

Read about remarkable people in all walks of life—not just the great and good, but those who left a mark, be they good, bad, or bizarre.

Browse through more than 10,000 portrait illustrations— the largest selection of national portraiture ever published.

Regular features on history in the news—with links to biographies—provide fascinating insights into topical events.

Get a life ... by email

Why not sign up to receive the free *Oxford DNB* 'Life of the Day' by email? Entertaining, informative, and topical biographies delivered direct to your inbox—a great way to start the day.

Find out more at www.oxforddnb.com

'An intellectual wonderland for all scholars and enthusiasts'

Tristram Hunt, *The Times*